Nigerian Administration and its Political Setting

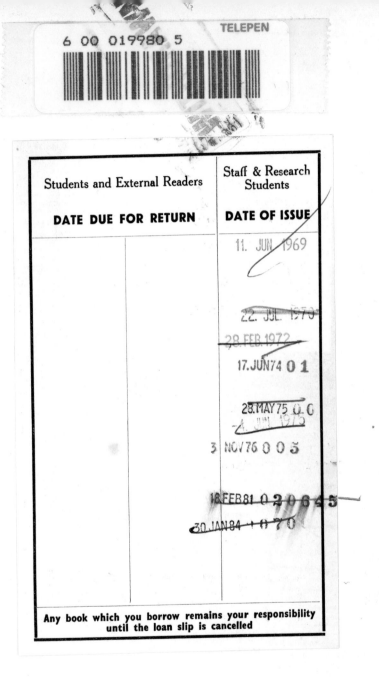

Nigerian administration and its political setting

A collection of papers given at the Institute of Administration, University of Ife, and edited by Adebayo Adedeji

Published for the

Institute of Administration, University of Ife, Nigeria by

HUTCHINSON EDUCATIONAL

HUTCHINSON EDUCATIONAL LTD
178–202 Great Portland Street, London W1

London Melbourne Sydney
Auckland Bombay Toronto
Johannesburg New York

First published 1968

This book has been set in Imprint, printed in Great Britain on Smooth Wove paper by Anchor Press, and bound by Wm Brendon, both of Tiptree, Essex

09 088620 8 (cased)
09 088621 6 (paper)

Contents

CONTENTS

vi

vii

Preface

When the Institute offered a programme of nine weekly lectures and symposia on the interactions of politics and administration in Nigeria for senior officers of governments and corporations from February to April 1966 it was not intended that the texts would be published. But the lectures were acclaimed to be of such a remarkably high standard and the programme itself, which was a star-studded one, received such enthusiastic support that it has been decided to accede to the popular demand to publish them so that they may reach a wider audience within and outside Nigeria. My only regret is that it has not been possible to publish a summary of the very lively discussions which followed each of the lectures and symposia.

The programme involved a large number of senior officials of the federal and regional governments, who, in spite of their heavy official commitments at a time when Nigeria had just witnessed a sudden change of government, took active part either as speakers, as chairmen of one of the nine sessions or as participants in the subsequent discussions. In all, over one hundred senior civil servants participated. Senior officials of federal and regional statutory corporations and members of the faculties of the Universities of Ife and Ibadan also took part.

I am most grateful to all the participants. In particular, I am indebted to P. T. Odumosu, MFR, Secretary to the Military Government and Head of the Western Nigeria Public Service; C. S. O. Akande, Chief Civil Engineer in the Ministry of Works and Transport; Chief J. M. Beckley, OON, Permanent Secretary, Ministry of Local Government; Dr G. A. Jawando and J. H. Price, both of the Faculty of Social Sciences in the University of Ife, who took turns at presiding over the sessions. My sincere thanks also go to all the contributors, without whose active cooperation and support this publication could not have seen the light of day.

Finally, I wish to express my gratitude to all my colleagues and former colleagues at the Institute, particularly to Dr Israel O. Ola and David Fauri, formerly Research Fellow and Associate Research Fellow respectively, and to Dr D. J. Murray, Senior Research Fellow and Research Director, for their assistance in organising the programme and in the editorial work. I am also grateful to Mr Dickson Agidee, the Institute's Librarian, who assisted in preparing the index. Let me hasten to add that, as editor, I assume full responsibility for any errors which may be found in this volume.

I have no doubt that the civil servants and officials of public corporations who took part in the programme will be glad to see the texts of the lectures in permanent print. It is also my hope that the other officials of the Nigerian governments who did not have the opportunity of participating in the programme, as well as the higher civil servants of the other African governments, will find this volume of interest and value. Unfortunately, it was not possible for any of the Nigerian politicians to take part in the programme, either as speakers or as participants. Their exclusion was not deliberate, but due to the circumstances of the time. I do hope, however, that as many of them as possible will find time to read these papers. They will find in them the views of higher civil servants on the past role of the politicians in administration, and suggestions about their future role and responsibility. I have no doubt that scholars, teachers and students of public administration and allied disciplines will find the book useful. If it spurs them to undertake further study of the interactions of politics and administration in the developing countries of Africa, it will have achieved its purpose.

I should perhaps hasten to add, on behalf of the civil servant contributors, that nothing contained in their papers should be taken as reflecting the official views of their governments or corporations. I should also like to add on behalf of my Institute that the views expressed are those of the authors and are not necessarily shared by the Institute.

Since this programme of lectures and symposia on the Nigerian administration within its political context was held, the country has witnessed another coup, a series of civil disturbances and a civil war to preserve the national integrity. The most far-reaching development is the creation of twelve states out of the former four regions and the federal territory of Lagos. The first move towards the restoration of the civilian régime has also been undertaken by the appointment of civilians into the cabinets of the federal and state governments. But the various problems and issues discussed in this volume are still as topical today as they were on January 15th 1966, when the first coup overthrew the civilian régime of the first Nigerian Republic.

Adebayo Adedeji
Institute of Administration, University of Ife

Part I

The frame of reference

1

Introduction: the evolution, organisation and structure of the Nigerian civil services

Adebayo Adedeji

The take-over of the governments of the Federal Republic of Nigeria by the armed forces after the *coup d'état* of January 15th 1966, brought to an end, at least for a season, the fourteen-year-old direct involvement of professional politicians in the administration of the country. Politicians began to participate directly in the administration of Nigeria in 1952, consequent upon the introduction in that year of a new constitution, commonly called the Macpherson Constitution after the then Colonial Governor of Nigeria, Sir John Macpherson, who initiated the process which culminated in the constitutional changes. Although a few Nigerians had been members of the colonial legislative and/or executive councils which had existed in the country since 1922, it was not until 1952 that Nigerians became intimately connected with the executive arm of government. In that year a number of the newly elected members of the central and regional legislatures set up under the constitution were appointed ministers of state. These politicians had contested elections to the regional and central legislatures on the platform of one political party or the other or had later enrolled as members of such parties.

But the involvement of the ministers of state in the administration of the country was extremely circumscribed under the 1952 Constitution. The ministers were given only collective responsibility as members of the central or regional cabinets over state matters. They were expected to leave the execution of government policy to the public officers who were invariably colonial administrators. They had no control whatsoever over the executive departments within their ministries.

The new ministers were soon frustrated by a situation where they could exercise only collective and not individual responsibility and power. As Chief Obafemi Awolowo, whose party, the Action Group, had formed the government of Western Nigeria put it in his autobiography:[1]

> Within four months of its introduction, the Action Group discovered a number of very serious defects in the Constitution. . . . The first defect we discovered was this. The Minister was to administer the affairs of his Department (not Ministry) in association with the official Head of that Department. We had interpreted this to mean that the Head of Department would only advise the Minister in regard to matters pertaining to his Department, and that if the Minister after due consideration made a decision, the Head of Department would, like a good civil servant, willingly and submissively abide by such a decision. But we soon discovered in practice that our construction was wrong and that a Minister was expected to be a junior partner in the departmental establishment. To us this was decidely unbearable. . . .

When the constitution proved unworkable in 1953 and a new one was introduced in October 1954 the ministers were given both collective and individual responsibility over the administration of their ministries. The cabinet system of government of the Westminster-Whitehall model was thus introduced into Nigeria. The 1957 constitutional changes which conferred self-government on both the Western and Eastern regions finally brought into being a fully fledged ministerial system in the two regions. Both the Northern regional government and the federal government soon followed the footsteps of the West and the East.

It was also the 1954 constitutional changes which turned Nigeria into a federation of three component parts and a federal

[1] *AWO—The Autobiography of Chief Obafemi Awolowo* (Cambridge University Press, 1960), pp. 232-3

territory. Consequent upon this constitutional development, the Nigeria Public Service was split into four public services—a Federal Public Service and three Regional Public Services, one for each of the three regions. Thus the granting of full ministerial powers to Nigerian ministers coincided with the establishment of regional as well as federal public services.

The development of the Nigerian Civil Services

When the Protectorate of Northern Nigeria and the Colony and Protectorate of Southern Nigeria were amalgamated on January 1st 1914, to form modern Nigeria, a single civil service was not immediately set up for the whole country. The North and South continued to be governed as they had been before 1914. The founder of Nigeria, Sir Frederick (later Lord) Lugard, resisted all attempts at centralisation and assimilation. The administrative areas of Northern and Southern Nigeria were placed under two Lieutenant-Governors, each with a secretariat and departmental organisation of its own. Only those departments which were practically indivisible and whose functions applied to the whole of Nigeria (Judiciary, Military, Railways, Posts and Telegraphs, and Audit) were centralised under the direct control of the Governor-General, assisted by a central secretariat. The only unifying factor was that all the officers were colonial civil servants.

Although a Nigerian civil service emerged during the 1920s, the postwar constitutional developments necessitated a great deal of administrative devolution to the regional administration set up in 1946 under the Richards Constitution.[1] The tripartite objective of that constitution was 'to promote the unity of Nigeria; to provide adequately with that unity for the diverse elements which make up the country; and to secure greater participation by Africans in the discussion of their own affairs'.[2]

To achieve the second objective, Nigeria was divided into three

[1] The Constitution was named after its author, the then governor of Nigeria, Sir Arthur Richards (later Lord Milverton)
[2] *Political and Constitutional Future of Nigeria*, the Governor of Nigeria's Despatch to the Secretary of State for the Colonies dated December 6th 1944. Sessional Paper No. 4 of 1945 (Government Printer, Lagos, 1945), p. 2

regions, and a Regional Council was set up in each region. A considerable measure of financial and administrative responsibility was devolved on the regional councils, and in order to ensure the effective performance of their tasks, adequate administrative machinery was provided at each regional headquarters. Each of the principal departments was regionalised and posts of regional deputies were created.

Thus, between 1946 and 1954, the central and unitary character of the Nigerian public service was considerably modified by delegation to the regional administration of certain powers of appointment, promotion, posting and discipline. Various services which were all-Nigerian in theory became regional services in practice. But, in spite of this, the unitary character of the Nigerian civil service was a fact of great significance. It was not until 1954, when the country became a federation, that this unitary civil service was replaced by the federal and three regional civil services—each of which was autonomous within its sphere of competence.

When the Mid-West region was created out of the Western region in 1963, it too established its own civil service. Thus, by the time of the military take-over of the country's administration, Nigeria had five civil services—a federal civil service and four regional civil services. With the creation of twelve states out of the four regions and the federal territory of Lagos in May 1967, the country now has thirteen civil services—a federal civil service and twelve state civil services.

Organisation and structure of the civil services

It cannot be the object of this chapter to examine the entire complex of the organisational problems of the Nigerian public services. We shall confine ourselves to a consideration of their administrative structures, for the purpose of pinpointing the basic weaknesses in the set-up. It is in the national interest that these structures should be reviewed. Indeed, one of the problems confronting all the new states of Africa in the area of public administration has been how to transform a colonial bureaucracy into a national civil service. It is a mistake to think that with the replacement of expatriate officers by Africans this transformation has been achieved.[1]

The structures of the regional and federal public services are very much alike. Each service is divided into the following three broad classes:

(1) the general service classes comprising
   (a) the administrative class
   (b) the general executive class
   (c) the secretarial/stenographic classes
   (d) clerical, messengerial and miscellaneous classes

(2) the specialist classes made up of people with a wide range of professional, scientific and technical qualifications, including ancillary technical staff

(3) departmental classes consisting of posts which are peculiar to particular departments, e.g. nurses, health inspectors, tax officers

The pattern of organisation adopted in the Nigerian public services is similar to that of the British civil service. There are ministries and non- or extra-ministerial departments. The number of ministries and their functions have varied from one public service to another. The tendency during the civilian régime has been a proliferation of ministries. For example, the number of ministries in Western Nigeria by the time of Independence in 1960 was twelve. By January 15th 1966 it had increased to nineteen. Increases in the scope of governmental activities cannot alone account for this increased number of ministries. Partisan political factors, and particularly the need to accommodate their political colleagues, led the heads of governments in the post-Independence period to create more and more ministries.

The question then arises whether there are any principles of

[1] J. D. Kingsley, 'Personnel Administration and Training', one of the technical papers presented at the Seminar of the Economic Commissions for Africa on *Urgent Administrative Problems of African Governments*, Feb.–March 1963, pp. 117–35

organisation which should govern the establishment of ministerial departments. Two such principles—both of them easy to formulate, though less easy to apply—come to mind. First, ministerial departments should correspond with distinct, functionally defined, administrative tasks. From this point of view one may ask whether it is logical to separate the administration of agriculture and natural resources from that of fisheries and forestry, or of cooperative and community development from that of agriculture and natural resources. Yet in 1966, the Government of Western Nigeria did establish separate ministries for each of these groups of functions. In the North, to give another example, separate ministries were created for agriculture, for animal and forest resources, for social welfare and cooperatives, and for health.

The second principle which should govern the creation of ministries is the availability or otherwise of qualified administrative personnel and financial resources. The dearth of both factors makes it advisable to keep the number of ministries low by assigning to each of them a fairly wide area of substantive jurisdiction.

Under the parliamentary system of government each ministry was headed by a minister who was responsible to the legislature for the functions and subjects within his portfolio. Ministers were both the political and executive heads of the ministries. However, certain matters such as appointments, promotions and discipline of civil servants were excluded from their purview by the Constitution. These were made the responsibility of the Public Service Commissions, in order to ensure an impartial civil service uninfluenced by political considerations. The Public Service Commissions, which are vested with these functions by the constitutions of the federation and of the regions, are, however, appointed by the heads of governments who are politicians.

The Permanent Secretary is the administrative head of the ministry. He is also the accounting officer. In the former capacity he is responsible to the minister and in the latter capacity he is directly responsible to the Public Accounts Committee of the federal parliament, or the regional legislature as the case may be. As the White Paper on the Reorganisation of Ministries in Western Nigeria Public Service puts it:

The Permanent Secretary, as Accounting Officer, is responsible both to the Legislature through the Public Accounts Committee and to the Minister, but this dual responsibility is not inconsistent. The Permanent Secretary answers to the Public Accounts Committee as to a judicial body which may examine him but take no responsibility for his actions or give him orders. The Legislature itself can act on the reports of the Public Accounts Committee by action directed to the Minister. The Permanent Secretary's responsibility to the Minister, on the other hand, is not judicial but administrative; he acts on behalf of and in the name of the Minister. His acts commit the Minister and he must answer to him for what he has done on his behalf.

Each ministry is divided into a number of divisions. The number of divisions depends on the range of functions for which the ministry is responsible. Within each ministry there is a division which is primarily responsible for financial control, accounting for expenditure and stores, establishments and organisation matters. This division, which is usually called *Administration and General Division*, is responsible for the overall management of the ministries, and it relieves high-ranking professional and administrative staff of the day-to-day routine administration. The other divisions are organised on a functional basis. For example, the Ministry of Works and Transport in the West has five divisions, as follows: Administration and General, Building, Highways, Water Supplies, and Mechanical and Electrical. The Ministry of Education has seven divisions—Finance and Establishments, Education Administration, Students and Special Services, Registration and Assessment, Examinations, Inspectorate and Technical Education. Each division is subdivided into branches, sections and subsections.

Thus each ministry is organised hierarchically, in addition to each of the Nigerian public services being organised on a class basis. The hierarchical and class structure of the Nigerian public services is indeed a British legacy. When the parliamentary system of government was introduced into Nigeria in the early fifties the structure of the British civil service was copied. Whatever may have been the experience in Britain, it is doubtful if such a structure is suitable to the needs of a developing nation like Nigeria, where the public sector plays a direct and dominant role in the developmental effort.

A public service organised hierarchically tends to reduce administration to a routine process. Papers are passed from subordinates to their superior officers, who in turn are content to pass orders accordingly or to forward them to their own superiors. The same routines tend to be followed too closely, regardless of the nature or importance of the issue under examination. The result is that many administrators do not operate at a level commensurate with their responsibility, with a consequent dearth of programme and policy initiative at top levels. If Nigeria is to achieve rapid economic and social development, and if the governments of the republic are to play their role in this process, the country's public services should be organised in a less hierarchical and less class-conscious way.[1]

Inter-class conflicts in the civil services

Inter-class conflicts, particularly those between the generalist administrators and the professionally qualified officials, plague the services. Before the federalisation of the civil services in 1954 and for some years thereafter, government departments were under the control of professional officers. Although an 'Administrative Service' had been in existence in the Nigeria civil service, the administrative officers in that service were primarily engaged in provincial administration as residents and district officers. The executive departments were headed by professional officers who were designated 'Directors' or 'Controllers'. The public service had by that time been viewed as consisting not of different classes or cadres but of two broad divisions—'senior' and 'junior' services.

It was the Gorsuch Commission, which was appointed in 1954 to look *inter alia* into the structure of the civil services, that

[1] See 'The Public Service and the Administration of Development Programmes in Nigeria' in the *Nigerian Journal of Economic and Social Studies*, Vol. 6, No. 3, November 1964, pp. 321–31, where the author has developed this theme at some length

recommended their reconstitution into three broad classes.[1] Consequent upon the acceptance of these recommendations by the Nigerian governments, the executive departments were integrated into ministries and members of the administrative class were appointed to the headship of the ministries.

These developments have resulted in a drastic change in the role of the professional officer *vis-a-vis* the administrative officer. Members of the administrative classes have emerged as the *corps d'élite* of the services. They are directly responsible to the ministers for the formulation of policies and for ensuring their proper and most effective execution. It is to this group of officers that ministers look for advice and help. They are therefore nearer to the politicians' minds, nearer to their points of view, than are the members of the other classes.

The pre-eminence of the administrative officer in the hierarchy of the public services in Nigeria is deeply resented by members of the professional classes. The inter-class conflicts and antagonisms which have ensued have led to a dissipation of energy and a waste of scarce resources. This has tended to reduce the ability of these two classes to perform their functions efficiently. Although inter-class conflicts do exist in the British civil service, it is doubtful if they are as intense as they are in the Nigerian public services.

The professional specialists hold the view that in executive ministries, like Works, Transport, Housing, Agriculture, etc., the advance of modern technology and the increasing complexity and diversity of the State's functions make it very difficult for anyone but a specialist to be in real command of the job. In many countries the concept of generalist administrators as it has developed in the United Kingdom and other Commonwealth countries is foreign. In these countries there is no administrative class *per se*, although there are administrators. Top-level permanent administrators in such countries are specialists involved in administration rather than generalist administrators.[2]

[1]L. H. Gorsuch, *Report of the Commission on the Public Services of the Governments in the Federation of Nigeria, 1954–55* (Government Printer, Lagos, 1955)
[2]F. D. McGrath, *The Role of the Administrator* (Recruitment and Training Division, The Treasury, Ibadan), January 1963, p. 5

2

The impact of politics on administration

D. J. Murray

The purpose of this paper is to consider the impact of politics on administration in Nigeria. Succeeding papers will develop certain themes arising from this general topic. So my aim is not to attempt a comprehensive survey of the question but to consider the background to it and to suggest the context for some of the specific issues which will be discussed in later papers. In doing this, rather than trying to make generalisations to cover the somewhat different circumstances of the separate regions and the federal government, I wish to concentrate on the particular situation in the Western region.

The focus of our attention in this series is the Administration. Some would prefer to call it the bureaucracy, but since this word has pejorative overtones many will take exception to the term and I will therefore avoid it. Whichever term is used, however, it describes the same individuals and institutions. It covers the formally organised offices which are grouped into sections, branches, divisions, departments, ministries, and the administrations in the four regions of the country and in the federal government at Lagos; and it is also concerned with the individuals who fill these offices and who are classified in the different grades of the general service and specialist classes. In the Western region this covers approximately 15,000 persons (excluding daily paid labour), and rather more offices, since there are established posts that remain unfilled. The population of the region, according to the 1963 population census, is approximately 10·5 million.

The Administration in the regions and federal government have found themselves deeply intertwined with politics. Before, however, explaining the nature of this involvement in politics, I wish first to explain the different senses in which we are accustomed to hear the term politics being used. It will, I think, facilitate our discussion of the issues if we start from a common understanding of the term.

The primary point is that popular usage tends to be different from academic usage, and to differ from society to society. It describes particular sorts of activities and frequently also carries overtones of approval or disapproval. In Tanganyika and Kenya, for instance, the Swahili word used to translate politics tended to convey the idea that politics was action against the government: 'politics is the disturbance of local and central government, by refusing to obey the law, pay poll-tax . . . politics means striking for higher wages'.[1] In northern Sierra Leone, a couple of years ago, Limba-speaking people had taken the word 'politics' into their language, and to them its primary meaning was the business of getting rich quick through government at the expense of people like themselves. Both on the Swahili Coast and among the Limba-speakers particular activities, though different sorts of activity, were regarded as being characteristic of 'politics'. If I may venture to suggest the Yoruba equivalent, I believe that the term used in Yoruba to describe politics is *oshelu*. Literally this means 'shaping or organising the town', and a person who engages in politics is an *awon oshelu*. But if you were to point to a particular civic dignitary and describe him as *awon oshelu* you would promptly be asked 'which party?'. What, in fact, the term *oshelu* describes in current usage is the activities of the various political parties—the Action Group (A.G.), the National Council of Nigerian Citizens (N.C.N.C.), the Nigerian National Democratic Party (N.N.D.P.), and the Northern Peoples Congress (N.P.C.). In other words, in popular parlance among Yoruba speakers politics is concerned with the activities of political parties.

[1] Quoted in W. Whiteley, 'Political Concepts and Connotations', in K. Kirkwood (ed.), *St Anthony's Papers Number 10, African Affairs*, Chatto and Windus, London, 1961, p. 14

Distinct from the popular uses of the term in different societies, 'politics' has a more academic use. Here it describes all activity that is concerned with securing the exercise of power in society. The classic exposition so far as contemporary academics are concerned is that given by Max Weber—' "politics" for us means striving to share power or striving to influence the distribution of power either among states or among groups within a state . . . . When a question is said to be a political question . . . what is always meant is that interests in the distribution, maintenance, or transfer of power are decisive for answering the question . . . .'[1] Some, instead of speaking of the exercise of power, prefer nowadays to say 'the allocation of authoritative values', but whatever one's preference, the point is that the term 'politics' covers a far wider range of activities, and many more individuals and groups, than the popular usages considered above.

In the academic sense, moreover, politics is inseparable from the activities of the Administration. Between politics and administration as functions, it is possible to postulate a distinction: to say that politics is concerned with deciding on the exercise of power, and administration with executing decisions. But these functions cannot then be regarded as belonging exclusively to distinct structures or institutions. Parliament or the legislature may have a predominant concern with politics—that is, with taking major decisions—but the Administration is deeply involved with formulating policy, and is concerned constantly with determining how discretionary authority should be used in particular circumstances. The fallacious idea that administering belongs exclusively to the public administration, and conversely that public administration is separated from politics is one that, in so far as it is accepted, derives from the American civil service reformers of the late nineteenth and early twentieth centuries. These reformers were concerned that there should be such a separation so that American public administration could be purged of 'the poisonous atmosphere of civil government, the crooked secrets of state administration, the confusion, sinecurism, and corruption ever and

[1] H. H. Gerth and C. Wright Mills, *From Max Weber, Essays in Sociology*, Routledge and Kegan Paul, London, 1948, p. 78

again discovered in the bureaux in Washington', as Woodrow Wilson put it in 1887. The reformers sought to limit the sphere of activity of the party politicians and to widen the area in which the public administration could act independently, but their own political platform does not provide a sure base for arguing for a logical separation between the function of politics and the activities of the institution called the Administration. Politics and administration may be separable as functions—though there are problems even in this idea—but it is fallacious to argue from this that the institution called the Administration is concerned exclusively with the function of administration and indeed that it alone is concerned with administering. In fact, the Administration is of necessity involved in politics.

Nevertheless, the nature of the impact of politics on the Administration is not something that can be discovered from a discussion of terms, nor will it be the same in all societies. We are particularly concerned with the impact of politics, in the wider sense, on the Nigerian Administration, and indeed on that in Western Nigeria. We are interested in how politics in Nigerian societies impinges on the working of the Administration, and how similarly it is affected by the politics within the Administration.

The first characteristic of politics in relation to the Administration in Western Nigeria is its intensity. The Administration is the focus of a great deal of political activity; it is subjected to constant and insistent demands from a wide range of interests and from many individuals. Letters, telephone calls, telegrams, personal callers pour in requesting interviews; messages, in one form or another, press particular causes; public meetings and newspaper comments are used to air demands and criticise decisions or inactivity. There is no need for me to elaborate the point that a great deal of political activity in this society is directed to trying to induce one part or other of the Administration to act in a desired way.

This intense political activity focussing on the Administration stems self-evidently from what is expected of government by society, and it is a characteristic of the last twenty years that government has been pressed to provide an increasingly wide range of amenities and services to the public. Twenty or so years ago, the citizens of Ogbomosho were pressing the government to provide the town with a communal wireless set powered by rechargeable batteries, to have gutters cemented by the Public Works Department, to equip the waterworks with a second pump, to have sons of Ogbomosho trained as sanitary overseers, and to station an Assistant District officer in the town. Since then the demands have increased—individual applications for loans, increased employment for sons of the town, a large teak plantation, more primary schools, telephone and telegraph services at the local post office, flyproofed market stalls, secondary schools, tarred roads including a new bypass, electricity supplies, a new reservoir and water supply, and most recently major industrial enterprises. These are only examples, but they indicate that the demands have been for increasingly costly and large scale developments. It is also that the number of demands has grown. There has, in other words, been a rapidly rising level of expectations in Ogbomosho, and there is, of course, nothing peculiar about that town.

The reasons for this rising level of expectations are various. In part, it was that after the second world war the colonial government had more money to spend—derived from the marketing boards, increased revenue and overseas aid—and it was concerned to spend this money on schemes of social and economic improvement; and, with money available, demand was quick to develop. Fresh expectations were also a by-product of the campaign for national independence. Politicians encouraged expectations in order to build up discontent against colonial government and so provide themselves with a basis of power. The growth of expectations has also been a result of improved communications, a more literate public, a wide circulation of newspapers, more people travelling and yet maintaining close links with their home towns, magazines, the transistor revolution, the introduction of commercial television—the means for stimulating demand has greatly increased in the twenty odd years since the people of Ogbomosho sought their single communal wireless set.

From our point of view, the reasons for this rising level of expectations are less important than its existence and the effects that it has had. Yet it is partly the reasons for it which explain why the focus for demands is the government, and within the government the Administration. The events of the last twenty odd years have not simply served to increase demands; it is expected that these should be met by government. This is partly because the colonial administration stimulated demands in order to spend the money available to it. It directly encouraged native authorities and later local councils, and even individuals, to put forward development schemes to be financed by the government. And when Chief Samuel Ojo received a loan of £250 to erect a corn mill at Shaki, Mr—as he then was—D. S. Adegbenro £800 for his piggery, and the Oshogbo Native Authority £1,960 for a teak plantation, others were prompted to expect similar help from the Administration. A further reason was that politicians focussed attention on what the government was not doing to meet the needs of the people. By rallying people behind a particular nationalist party, because of the shortcomings of colonial rule, politicians were helping to encourage the idea that it was the responsibility of the government to provide the particular benefits currently being denied to people.

There are two further circumstances that help to explain why it is civil servants within government who are the focus of attention. In the first place, there is the tradition created by the office of district officer. Under colonial rule, in the absence effectively of representative participants in government, the district officer was the primary channel of communication between the people of a district and the government. He was the agent of government with an all-embracing responsibility for his district, and he was regarded as the means of access to government authority—hence of course the concern of Ogbomosho to have an assistant district officer in the town. Since 1955 the Western Nigeria government has been abolishing the offices of Residents and District Officers, and substituting for them a system under which each ministry maintains its own field agents. Yet the role of district officers, while formally abolished, lives on in the minds of many citizens. Field agents and pre-eminently the local government advisers, as the successors of the district officers, are regarded not simply as the executive agents of government, but also as channels of communication and the means of access to the power of the government.

To some extent this prevailing attitude to officials is not simply a relic of the colonial past but a reflection of the distribution of power in the state. Officials in Western Nigeria, as in other states, are recognised as having a part to play in policy formation, and they are known to exercise discretionary authority.

There is, therefore, a high level of expectations in this society, and the belief that government can and should satisfy demands. Many of these demands are addressed to civil servants, and this means that, in the wider sense of the term politics, the civil servants are the focus of considerable political activity.

The position occupied by civil servants, and particularly by those in the administrative class, has helped to accentuate the difficulties of civil servants in another sphere of politics. This concerns their relations with the ministers, and with both the Assembly and extra-Assembly party organisations. The administration in Western Nigeria has been operating in a climate of intense inter-party competition since elections to the Regional Assembly were first held in 1951. The details of the inter-party struggles do not concern us; the point is that at no time since 1951 has one party achieved an overwhelmingly dominant and secure position in the region. From 1956 to 1962 the Action Group came closest to a dominant position, but then that party was rent in two, and since then the conflict between the newly formed Nigerian National Democratic Party and the Action Group has become increasingly bitter, unscrupulous and violent.

This party political situation has had a marked effect on the Administration. Arising from the fact that it has been the focus of demands from individuals and groups in society, the Administration has been deeply concerned with the formulation of government policy. In this, it has of course been further encouraged through a commitment to the development of the particular services for which different civil servants are responsible. Veterinary Officers are personally committed to controlling cattle diseases, Medical Officers of Health to removing dangers to health, and so on. Yet administrators have found themselves up against the party political interests of ministers.

The party interests of ministers have led them to be concerned, in the first place, with the allocation of resources to suit party political objectives. Development schemes of all sorts have been used as a reward for the faithful, and the denial of these resources has been the instrument for encouraging communities attached to an opposition party to change its allegiance. The Action Group government in the region, for instance, deprived the city of Ibadan of a share in the distribution of government resources because of its support for the National Council of Nigerian Citizens under Alhaji Adegoke Adelabu. Politically this policy paid off, for by 1961 the vast majority of voters had switched their support to the Action Group. Nevertheless, in so far as civil servants had to deal with representations from groups in the city, and were themselves committed to trying to prevent outbreaks of plague or ensuring that water continued to flow through the pipes, they were in conflict with the ministers. Yet up to 1962 it appears that the genuine enthusiasm of the ruling party for promoting economic and social development ensured that in general there were harmonious relations between administrators and ministers.

The major difficulties in the relations of ministers and senior civil servants have arisen since 1962 and have stemmed in large part from the preoccupation of ministers and of the ruling party with maintaining its position in power. Where, before 1962, the distribution of resources for party political purposes was counterbalanced by a sincere commitment to advancing the social and economic well being of the community, since the crisis in that year there has been a single-minded concern with maintaining power. The presumption in a representative political system is that the rulers safeguard their support among the electorate by formulating and executing policies that are acceptable to a majority of the electorate. The ruling party since 1962 has not, however, been content with such an indirect approach to its objective. In general terms, policy has not been formulated on the basis of promoting development and, as a result, ensuring a contented electorate; rather, decisions have been taken more explicitly on the basis of how many votes will this buy or how large a contribution will this secure for party or personal funds. This was the sort of question which most civil servants regarded as beyond their field of responsibility. Their concern was with the development of agriculture or industry, or the efficient use of the region's limited financial resources. Ministers and civil servants have therefore been seeking to achieve different objectives, and one consequence of this has been that ministers have tended to ignore their senior civil servants in taking the major decisions on policy in their ministries.

Difficulties in securing the cooperation of ministers and civil servants in formulating policy derive, of course, from other factors also—one being the attitude of some civil servants. Officials are given on occasion to suggesting that they know better than their ministers. This appears to be the case particularly where officials have, or pretend to have, a technical mastery of a subject that ministers do not share. Minutes full of the lawyer's jargon pass to a minister—minutes speaking of the *modus operandi* and *functus officio*—or a decision is expected, on the basis of the technical specifications, about which of two machines is more suitable. Such attitudes and practices have bred mistrust among ministers, and have reduced the possibility of a harmonious working relationship between ministers and civil servants. Ministers' party political objectives are, in other words, not the only cause of difficulties in the relations of ministers and civil servants, but they are one, and are particularly relevant to the immediate point with which we are concerned—namely, the impact of party politics on the Administration.

This lack of harmony between political heads and civil servants has, furthermore, affected the conduct of more routine administration. Just as major decisions have tended to be dictated by narrowly political objectives, so has the conduct of administration. In the eyes of party politicians, the purpose of administration has been to achieve direct party political objectives, whatever the ostensible purpose of the action. Let me give an example. The Housing Corporation has ostensibly been concerned to build houses that are habitable and command acceptable rents. Contracts were awarded, and it then became the responsibility of officials of the corporation to check that work was being executed according to the stipulated specifications; yet in trying to do this officials were confronted by a link between certain contractors and the political party, and through the party between contractors and appropriate government-appointed functionaries, so that any attempt to enforce the stipulated specifications tended to be disapproved by the functionaries in charge of the corporation. Contractors' financial support for the party was more important than building safe and habitable houses. Other examples could be given that relate to other areas of government activity, but I trust that the point is clear: politicians have been directly interested in the conduct of the details of administration. They have been concerned to ensure that their immediate objectives are served of building up the strength of the party and of their personal following within it, and of retaining power in the region. Yet the ostensible purpose for the administrative action is the one with which administrators have been concerned. Thus in the administration of policy, just as in its formulation, the interests of administrators and party politicians have diverged.

Another related point, and one that further explains the interest of ministers in the details of administration, is that administrators tend to assume that the techniques of administration which they use are politically neutral. It is the belief that what is regarded as the right way for an administrator to behave—the way that is in some regards laid down in general orders—will also be regarded by the public as the correct way for administrators to act. Administrators are committed, for instance, to acting on the basis of the law and subordinate legislative instruments of Western Nigeria, and they are committed to treating all on the basis of equality. Neither of these principles is necessarily accepted by sections of the public. In applying the law on chieftaincy succession, for instance, administrators are required to act according to the chieftaincy declarations in determining how a new chief shall be selected and who is eligible as a candidate. Yet frequently, in the eyes of those concerned, a literal application of the law in this case amounts to flouting the customary law which they believe should be paramount. It would appear that on the whole party politicians are more sensitive to the beliefs of the people in this regard than are

administrators, and, arising from this awareness, they are interested in the day to day conduct of administration, and are not
always sympathetic to the values which administrators regard it as
their duty to uphold in their conduct of administration.

For several reasons, therefore, there has been a lack of harmony
between the party political ministers and civil servants in the
Administration. In the last four years in particular, the Administration has not met what was immediately required of it by the
ministers, and one consequence of this has been that ministers
have been seeking to mould the Administration so that it meets the
party's requirements. Most recently, immediately before the coup,
the government had been planning to place the management of the
service under direct party political control. Previous to this,
ministers had sought to exploit the internal divisions within the
Administration in order to mould it more effectively to suit its
purpose.

It is in these circumstances that the internal politics within the
Administration have become so significant. The internal
divisions, and the struggles for power and influence within the
service, have provided an opportunity for party politicians to
attempt to refashion the Administration as a compliant instrument
of their will.

Within the Administration in Western Nigeria, as in all administrations, there is a considerable measure of internal political
activity. The most marked tensions and divisions within the service
in Western Nigeria derive from the fact that the service and the
Administration have only recently been refashioned. The different
classes have been created in their present form only since 1956.
The distribution of responsibilities—and the subordination of
professional officers to administrative class officers within newly
established ministries—date only from 1958. The major difficulties inherent in such drastic changes are only gradually being
worked out. In addition, there are the tensions between age-
groupings based on the relatively rapid promotion achieved by the
most senior administrative class officials during the period when
the service was being built up and administration expanded, and,
in contrast to this, the poor promotion prospects, at least in

B

relation to expectations, of most junior administrative class officials. Added to these are divisions which reflect those in the society of the region between those from the most southern areas, where education was available earlier, and those from else-where—who have in this regard an affinity with certain politicians recently in power. Also, as is common in many countries, there is inter-departmental rivalry which most notably is directed against the Treasury.

Nevertheless, these internal tensions would not be subjected to such consideration as they are, were it not for two circumstances. The first is the one already mentioned: the attempt on the part of the ruling politicians to mould the Administration as a direct instrument of their own. The second is the calibre and self-conscious pride of the members of the Administration. While speaking of divisions and tensions in the civil service, it has to be recognised that the civil service remains remarkably united and has a considerable *esprit de corps*. Much of this is due to the outstanding leadership provided by Chief Simeon Adebo, to the early replacement of expatriates so that a spirit of unity could emerge, to able personnel management in difficult conditions, and to the concentration of administrators at headquarters in Ibadan rather than their dispersal through provincial centres. We are not, however, concerned with considering the reasons for the quality of the service. It is the fact of it which is important, because were it not an able and efficient service, and if it did not have a spirit of unity and pride in its work, it would not be concerned to consider self-consciously and critically the problems that have confronted it, particularly during the past four years. In fact, senior civil servants are concerned to face the problems that have arisen: problems in the relations of administrators and out-side interests; the role of administrators in policy formulation; the respective roles of administrators and ministers; above all, how to eliminate internal conflicts in order to maintain a united civil service that has the capacity to withstand encroachments by party politicians.

Our interest in the general question of the impact of politics on administration derives from a practical concern over difficulties that have been experienced in recent years. I have concentrated, in discussing this question, on the Western region; conditions and circumstances in the other regions and in the Federal Government have in some respects been different, though difficulties experienced in the West have also been met with elsewhere. These difficulties, I have suggested, have been encountered in three broad areas. First, they derive from the activity of a wide range of groups and individuals in this society who are seeking benefits from the Administration; second, they stem from party politics; and third, and partly as a result of the second, they are due to the internal politics within the Administration. In discussing these issues we could, if we wished, draw on academic work in relation to other developing countries and contribute ourselves to contemporary debates, for academics have attempted to label and categorise different types of situations. They talk of agraria and industria, of prismatic societies where values agglutinate as they pass through prisms; they consider the appropriate words to describe the stages of bureaucratisation, but we are not concerned with contributing to debates about abstract terminology. We accept—I trust—that politics cannot be banished from the Administration, and what we are concerned to do is to face the practical problems that arise from the impact of politics on administration.

Part II

The Public, the politician and the administration

3

The politics of modernisation and its effect on the administration[1]

James O'Connell

This short paper takes for granted that the political intelligentsia of the African countries are not only politicians who compete with one another for power but statesmen who are interested in the use of power for the good of their countries. Similarly, the public servants of the different countries are men who devote a vast proportion of their working time to the affairs of the people whom they are meant to serve. But there are peculiar problems that face politicians and administrators in these newly independent and developing countries. And it is on these problems that this paper lays its stress.

The existing civil services in West Africa date from the colonial era. They antecede the growth of politics in the contemporary sense of democratic, secular and individualist competition for the right to rule. Though important political decisions were from time to time made in the metropolitan capitals, most colonial government consisted of rule in the different territories by expatriate civil

[1] A concept of modernisation is taken for granted in this paper. Modernisation is a process that includes the development of mental attitudes that look inventively for causal relations between happenings, and attitudes that seek to structure and control the flow of events through the historical understanding of time past and the planned uses of time ahead; it involves multiplying tools and machines in a society and imparting the skills or techniques needed to manipulate those technological instruments; and it requires social structures that become increasingly complex and differentiated, that demand advanced administrative capacity and that contain a built-in willingness to accept and initiate change.

servants who combined legislative, executive and judicial functions. With independence, not only does control of the state shift from foreigners to native-born individuals but—at least in principle—it shifts from bureaucrats to elected politicians. Yet the new states owe most of the social identity they possess as states to the previous unity of administration. When the small power group, which the nationalist politicians were, took over government, it was the professional administrators who maintained the continuity in the public services that underpinned the popular consent to be ruled. And, finally, it is the civil servants who have provided legal and functional continuity in those countries where the first lot of politicians have lost—sometimes violently—their title to legitimacy.

Politics and administration are concerned with improving social welfare, upholding law and order, and formulating and implementing foreign policy. Carrying out these tasks successfully is not easy in developing countries. Though the governments can draw on the new pride and loyalty that come with self-rule, the legitimacy of the new rulers remains fragile. The schools that have begun to spread and the standards of living that have begun to rise arouse expectations among large sections of the population. But expectations tend to grow faster than the economy can develop. The nationalist movement added a surge of sentiment to the social cohesion that the Administration had fostered between the ethnic groups of the colonial quasi-state. But political integration generally remains a problem after independence—and inter-ethnic rivalry and bitterness (tribalism) develop sharply in the course of the competitive modernisation of communities. Education imparts skills. But the schools are seldom geared to producing skills in the right proportions for the needs of the various sectors of the economy. Formal schooling also, allied with other social forces, sends youths into towns faster than the rudimentary facilities of those towns can handle. People learn to appreciate the value of money and accept the inducement of wages. However, traditional relationships break down or are inadequate for the new conditions, and there is haphazard mixing of individuals and groups in the new sectors of society. Human relations in this mixed and changing society are not predictable compared with traditional relationships. One consequence is that individuals seek security through accumulating money, and hence a corrosive and pervasive financial corruption spoils public and personal relationships. Finally, the new countries need, expect and seek foreign aid. But they want to reject the conditions attached and they dislike the dependence that it brings.

Involved in all the phenomena that we have been considering is a certain ambivalence about the past and the present, about tradition and the process of modernisation. A society that hurries from the hoe to the computer within a few short years cannot easily reconcile its history with the adaptations that the new situations impose. Tradition decays as the machines break through the arrangement of its social structures and as new values, secular and religious, modify personal and social priorities. Yet only through keeping up continuity with the past can a people retain its identity, maintain its self-respect, and even pass judgement on new techniques and values. Politicians and administrators alike struggle with these new situations. But it would be a mistake to envisage the politicians and the administrators as persons who cope with conditions external to themselves. These key organising groups are part and parcel of the changing conditions: they manifest in their own attitudes the ambivalence that marks the uneasy balance of tradition and modernity; they suffer the tensions that the uncertainties of social change create; and they possess little time or opportunity to reflect with detachment on their circumstances.

The politicians

Politicians are men who compete for power within the state; who deploy it to achieve goals embodying varying degrees of public welfare and private gain; and who nearly always want to retain power indefinitely. Most of the first political leaders of the new states are men who came up through the anti-colonial nationalist movements. These men, who once spent much of their time in agitational politics, are now confronted with the delicate handling of independence and the tangled problems of social modernisation.

These men have their first taste of power, and they have to deal with opponents whom they dislike and distrust. Yet they need to respect the 'rules of the game' (willed limitations on forms of competitiveness) without which they may destroy one another. They have yearned for years to take the place of the colonial masters. Yet they have to learn to accept a constitutional framework that seems designed to leave them much less powerful than the colonial régime. They love the adulation that surrounds ruling. Yet they need quickly to grasp that a sense of urgency in using power is vastly more important than the prestige of its possession. They were impressed in the past by the apparently ubiquitous and omnicompetent colonial bureaucracy. Yet they soon discover that this bureaucracy stretched thinly through the countryside and was (and remains) short of skills and money. They organise political parties that have little or no access to private funds in the way that parties have in developed countries. Yet the party organisers are judged by standards of public behaviour taken from the developed countries. The politicians have to be able to identify with, communicate with and draw on the values and support of traditional communities. At the same time they have to be able to detach themselves from communalism, its particularistic ethos and often static conditions, to reach a social identity and goals that are as wide as the entire political community and that depend on a technology and social organisation oriented to skills and merit.

Along with those tasks sketched in the previous paragraph—which might be said to demand multi-cultured individuals to deal with them—goes another set of problems that arise directly out of the circumstances of socio-economic development. Formal schooling arouses expectations that governments must meet to some extent if they are to survive. It is easy for a sense of relative deprivation to set in among large sectors of the educated elements in a developing country and for a revolution of rising expectations to go explosively sour in a revolution of rising frustrations. But if the task of leading the country towards economic growth falls on the political leaders, the latter have to try to buttress it with employment, spread its benefits over competing communities and reconcile in both justice and expediency the claims of town and country dwellers. And not the least challenge for the leaders is to inspire the mobilising elements of society with a vision of social achievement. At the same time they have to be able to persuade followers and opponents that they are not guilty of injustice or devoid of ability when the fulfilment of the vision is constantly deferred to the future.

The civil servants

The colonial civil servants were mainly concerned with maintaining law and order in the early years of colonisation. In the later years they began gradually to devote a growing part of their time and energies to expanding social welfare and directly promoting economic growth. Their successor-bureaucrats come under the control of politicians who are themselves under popular pressure to improve welfare and who have little sense of the financial cost involved. The bureaucrats find themselves given greatly extended commitments in economic development, education and health, not to mention the new security problems of independence. They themselves often have no more than a few years of administrative experience. They draw heavily on their formal schooling to work out solutions that convention and routine supply readily in other countries. And being heirs of the autocratic tradition of colonial bureaucracy, they almost always resent the overlordship of party politicians and they sometimes disdain, and seldom care to conciliate, the democratic sentiments of the traditional-minded communities.

The senior administrators are usually poorly supported by the intermediate cadres since the intermediate skills tend to be the least well provided for in the educational system. Yet the intermediate clerks and technicians are educated enough to appreciate the gulf that separates them from the senior levels and they eye with bitter resentment the status and emoluments of their superiors. Within the senior ranks the first arrived occupy the first places, and their relatively young years leave the later arrivals (sometimes abler and better qualified) little hope of the rapid promotions that the spiralling careers of their predecessors led them to expect for themselves. And for all the formal rules that govern promotions and transfers within the public service, the civil servants discover, and some exploit the fact, that not only do professional politicians interfere with the service but personal and communal rivalries also play a role within its ranks.

The single most crucial issue that tries bureaucrats is the strain they undergo as they endeavour to reconcile loyalty to their current political masters with the dispassionate integrity and scientific administrative procedures that safeguard the interests of the whole political community. The bureaucrats find their work for the political community made more complicated and their cooperation with the politicians more difficult because the latter who often possess no great amount of formal education distrust those who do. Finally, there is an ideological trauma that marks the relationship between the politicians and the bureaucrats. The bureaucrats have learned in the context of a dying Western nationalism to idealise their country. But it is very hard to do this when they often despise as ignorant, arbitrary and venal those political representatives who hold prior political rights to mould the image of the state within and to project it without. Only the best and most committed administrators can keep up their morale in the context of poor political leadership.

In their relations with the masses of the people the bureaucrats find within themselves two tendencies that are apt to run in opposite directions. They appreciate the understanding and the intimacy that common traditions and languages give them with the ordinary people whose affairs they administer—an understanding and intimacy that the colonial officials could acquire only with time and labour. Yet only reluctantly do they try to learn traditions other than those of their community of origin, and young officers are often less ready to bridge ethnic and educational differences than were the colonial officials. Also, sure of the cultural background to which they returned periodically and to which they could eventually withdraw, the colonial officers were willing to endure the human loneliness and cultural isolation of the bush; and most of them preferred service in the provinces to working in the secretariat. But most of the successor-bureaucrats intended in acquiring education to move away from the countryside—and later on in the service the incentives to move away are strengthened by the knowledge that promotions run more smoothly and frequently at the secretariat than out of sight in the field. Not least, the old colonials travelled light, often without wives, and usually without children, so it mattered little enough that amenities and schools were wanting where they lived. At this juncture there enters into consideration the entire question of the standard of living and remuneration of the senior administrators. They are the key organisational group in modernisation because they alone possess the skills that are necessary to the process. They need a standard of living within which those skills can be maintained and deployed. But inevitably it removes them from the under-housed, and sometimes chronically ill, traditional communities. There is some danger that their superior living conditions may render the administrators less sensitive than they should be to the urgency of bettering the lot of the masses. It may fall to the lot of other educated individuals in society, who possess the detachment that academic or other such positions give, to remind the administrators that a social conscience is a most vital possession in developing areas.

One last problem is worth mentioning. The urgency and originality of the social and technical situations that confront the new countries may well demand creative thinking and efforts. Yet their bureaucrats have been trained to administer and transmit established order rather than to innovate. And even those who would wish to innovate are driven to reflect that resources are too scarce to be gambled with and that developed countries possess much more room in which to experiment than do the underdeveloped.

Conclusion

In resolving issues like promoting creative leadership, fostering a sense of urgency in development, drawing up ordered forms of administration and putting forward the interests of the people generally, the politicians and the administrators meet in a common set of tasks in which there is distinction of gifts, division of powers and variety of skills. The politicians lead, and they are ultimately responsible to the people. But they need to be able to stimulate their administrators, evaluate their advice, and act cooperatively with them. The latter work out the technical implications of projects and execute policies. Political leadership without administrative and technical expertise is power in a vacuum; administration without political leadership is only tidiness in stagnation. Politics and administration belong together in the dynamics of a dialectical relationship. But there is no perfectly ordered model for this relationship, and no perfect delineation of responsibilities or functions will fit all the needs and possibilities of development.

4

Interest groups and administration in Nigeria

D. J. Murray

A cursory reading of the daily press is sufficient to show that interest groups play an active part in Nigerian government, and of these activities many civil servants are critical. My intention in this paper is to consider, first, the role of interest groups in Nigerian administration, and then to discuss some of the difficulties that are arising from this relationship.

The variety of interest groups operating in Nigeria could be illustrated by the representations made to General Ironsi in the weeks following the military coup of January 15th 1966. Letters of congratulation are reported to have come, among a great many others, from the Yam Traders' Association, Oluponna Youths Association, Eastern Nigeria Traders' Association, Nigeria Nurses' Association, Afokhai Family Union and Ogbomosho Descendants' Union. Other examples could be given of associations comprising members of a particular profession, trade or occupation, age groups, or people from a particular area or of a certain family. Whatever the basis of membership, they are all organised associations, concerned to safeguard the welfare of the particular group, and hence the general term 'interest group' is used to describe them.

Such interest groups as these play a significant part in the work of administration in this country. In the first place, many of them are seeking to gain benefits for their organisations from the government, and within government they are trying to induce administrators to exercise their authority or influence in a way that benefits their group. I will give two examples of interest groups as organisations bringing pressure to bear on the Administration in the country. First, the Lagos Chamber of Commerce is an active and powerful interest group that seeks benefits from Federal Government departments and corporations. As the Chamber states, 'its main functions are the protection of all matters affecting trade and industry for the promotion of the economic growth of the country'. It is an established body, with a continuing organisation, and firm links with government departments. It makes constant representations to the Ministry of Communications about the postal and telegraph system; its concern over the electricity supply situation is well known to the general manager of the Electricity Corporation; inefficient handling of cocoa at Apapa recently led to meetings with the chairman of the Western Nigeria Marketing Board and the Ministers of Transport, Trade and Economic Development; the Office of Statistics was persuaded to publish statistics more adequate to the needs of commerce and industry. The Chamber, in other words, maintains constant contact with a wide range of ministries and departments representing to them the needs and expectations of organised commerce.

As a contrast to the Lagos Chamber of Commerce one might take a family or lineage concerned to secure the selection of their candidate to fill a vacant chieftaincy in a particular town. To follow the course of a particular disputed election in the Western region shows the way the Administration here also is brought into contact with an interest group. During a chieftaincy election the first point of attention for contesting parties is the secretary of the relevant district council who has to receive nominations and prepare the papers for the Chieftaincy Committee. The next point of attention is the Kingmakers whose responsibility it is to select from among the candidates. After this stage the attention of rival lineages shifts from the local community to the Ministry of Chieftaincy Affairs, where it is for the officials to prepare a recommendation on the action to be taken by the Executive Council. The lineage successful at the meeting of the Kingmakers seeks to uphold the validity of earlier proceedings, while the unsuccessful one attempts to find grounds for urging that the election be set aside. The office receives a spate of letters, telegrams and demands for personal interviews; and then, with the papers prepared and recommendation decided on, attention shifts to the Executive Council. Finally, with the issue settled and confirmed by the Governor-in-Council, the interest groups that were called into being by the vacancy fade away once more.

There is a considerable difference between the Lagos Chamber of Commerce and a lineage, but they are both interest groups that direct their attention to the Administration. They both, like the many other interest groups active in the society, are seeking benefits for their organisation and its members. They concentrate their attention and efforts on those individuals and institutions that possess the power relevant to the ends they are seeking. Where such power is located depends on the ends sought: the power may belong to a district council, the local Ogboni Society or the Oba; to a civil servant, a minister, the legislature or elsewhere, but in Nigerian government, whether at the federal or regional level, since much discretionary authority belongs to civil servants, the Administration is inevitably the focus of considerable attention from interest groups.

The role of interest groups in administration, however, goes beyond making representations or bringing pressure to bear on the Administration. There is a reciprocal aspect to this relationship. Interest groups are seeking benefits from government, but equally the Administration is concerned to use interest groups to assist with the formulation and implementation of government policy.

To take policy formulation first, the rational conduct of public affairs requires that decisions should be taken on the basis of relevant information. Interest groups provide one source of such information. The information may be in the form of data about activities in the field where the interest group operates. The Lagos Chamber of Commerce, for instance, has its own Economics and Statistics Standing Committee. The Nigerian Employers' Consultative Association has undertaken surveys and collected statistics about the activities of its members, and these similarly are made use of by government departments. In addition to such data, however, interest groups provide information about the attitudes and opinion of members, and this also is necessary for a knowledgeable and rational approach to policy formulation. The role of interest groups as suppliers of information has been particularly important in recent years as the federal and regional governments have sought to widen the scope of government activity. By concerning themselves more fully with the problems of social and economic development, the governments have moved into areas where they lack a store of necessary information, and interest groups are in a position to assist by remedying deficiencies.

In the implementation of policy, interest groups similarly have a part: they are being used in a variety of ways as instruments for securing compliance with government policy. Where there is already popular demand for a particular type of development, the Administration is able to use relevant interest groups as a means of harnessing popular enthusiasm to the cause of implementing government policy. The progressive unions that exist in most towns in the Western region have been particularly important from this point of view. Take, for instance, the work of the Ogbomosho Parapo Federal Council in developing education in that town. The Parapo seeks to enroll all the sons of Ogbomosho and to enlist their support in developing the town, and one of its earlier objectives was to found an educational institute; but the Parapo's attention was directed to the need for secondary schools and as a result two schools financed by the Parapo have been built in the town. The Girls' High School was initiated with contributions from the Parapo's branches in the Northern region; the money for the Grammar School came initially from the branch of the Parapo in Ghana.

A second use to which interest groups are put by the Administration is as channels of communication and instruments of education. The Poultry Producers Association and the Cocoa Producers Union are both organisations that the Western Nigeria Ministry of Agriculture and Natural Resources has encouraged in order to provide the ministry with a way of disseminating information. Thus during the initial development of large scale poultry farming in the Ibadan circle, the existence of the Poultry Producers Association enabled meetings to be held between technical experts and producers. The members of the associations were obvious persons to whom to distribute the ministry's periodical, *The Poultryman's Companion*, and through the association contact could be maintained between extension officers and private producers in order that the former could learn, for example, of the requirements in day old chicks. In other words, by developing such organisations as these, the ministry is provided with a means of communicating with farmers, educating them in improved production methods, and learning of their requirements.

Interest groups serve in a further way as instruments for promoting compliance with government objectives. By introducing representative interest groups in the formulation of policy the Administration is helping to secure a climate of opinion favourable to resulting decisions. In part this is achieved through education. Such associated interest groups can see the reasons for a particular decision, but also, the different and possibly rival interests can meet together with officials, and thus provide an opportunity of devising a scheme that minimises conflicts with, and between, separate interests. This approach is used both in the preparation of policy in a general field and in the implementation of particular projects. An example of the first is provided by the machinery that exists for formulating educational policy in the Western region. A link with the principal interests involved in the development of education has been institutionalised through the Advisory Board on Education. On this are represented a wide range of organised bodies covering the teachers, churches, and school proprietors.

One example of the widely followed practice of consulting with affected interest groups on the implementation of particular policies is the consultation that has taken place between the Ministry of Agriculture in the Western region and the Ibadan butchers on the project for building a large modern abattoir for Ibadan. For some years the regional government has been intending to build this abattoir, and this, of course, affects the Ibadan butchers. Officials of the Ministry of Agriculture, however, have maintained a close contact with the Ibadan butchers' union, and in spite of the major changes the establishment of an abattoir would bring, the butchers have become enthusiastic supporters of the project—so much so that with delays occurring in the execution of the scheme the butchers have become an embarrassingly vocal and demanding pressure group.

Interest groups are, therefore, being extensively used in administration in this country. They play a part in collecting information necessary to the rational formulation of policy, and they form part of the machinery for implementing policy. Yet in spite of the role of interest groups in administration, they are in disfavour with civil servants, at least in the Western region. The opposition to interest groups and to their activities tends to be attributed to the idea that for interest groups to be associated with administrators subverts the principle of the Constitution that the legislature should be the focus of attention for representative bodies. Real as is the concern that pressure groups might be acting improperly, it seems clear that there are other circumstances that go further towards explaining civil service doubts about the propriety of the Administration being associated with interest groups.

There appear to be four closely related difficulties arising in the relations of public servants and interest groups. There is, first of all, the fear that policy formulated on the basis of consultations with interest groups does not accord with the public interest. In many societies the charge is made that civil servants think they are more effective guardians of the public interest than the public itself, and it could be argued that the public interest is only what results from the interaction of different groups. Yet it would seem that there is some substance behind the fears of civil servants in this society. In Nigeria not all interests are equally effectively represented: certain groups are well organised and act as powerful advocates of their own case, but civil servants are frequently up against the difficulty of being unable to find other interests to counteract the tendency for decisions to accord closely with the wishes of the single dominant interest group. In the opinion of some civil servants, this is the position in the field of educational administration, where the influence of the National Union of Teachers, both directly and through the churches, is not effectively balanced by other bodies, with the result that educational policy is considered to reflect too closely the interests of the Union.

A second difficulty runs parallel to the first. Many of the interest groups in the Western region, and in the country as a whole, are small and localised. Not only is it difficult to find groups to counterbalance such large ones as there are; it is also difficult in many fields to establish effective and fruitful relations with interest groups because the organisation, membership, and influence of existing interest groups are frequently confined to a single town or even to a ward or village. Had the Western Region Ministry of Trade and Industry a reason for seeking the cooperation of bicycle repairers in the region, or if the Nigeria Police sought to utilise hunters on a regional basis in their traditional role of night police, the largest organisations with which they could deal would be the separate bicycle repairers' and hunters' guilds that exist in the majority of towns in the region. The problem of establishing contact with these local interest groups seems to be particularly acute in the Western region, because here government has to a considerable extent dismantled the structure of local administration that is based on area—on the old districts under the all embracing authority of the district officer—preferring instead a functional division of responsibilities; yet local interest groups, in so far as they are integrated into larger organisations, are joined, not on a functional, but on an area basis: the bicycle repairers are not linked in a regional bicycle repairers association, but, rather, act as constituent associations within the different town progressive unions. The result, therefore, is that to some extent the basis of organisation in the regional government is inconsistent with that of a high proportion of interest groups.

Confronted with the difficulty of trying to make contact with a multiplicity of small local interest groups and establishing a cooperative working relationship with them, various ministries in this region have sought to encourage the formation of region-wide representative organisation; but this in turn has given rise to a further major difficulty. In the party political conditions of recent years, representative associations, created by the Administration for administrative purposes, have become the prey of party politicians. To some extent this would seem to derive from the fact that party politicians have been unsure of popular support and have lacked sufficiently effective differentiated party organisations to provide them with a secure basis of power in the state. They have, as a result, sought to attach all representative associations to their following. It also appears that to some extent the interest of party politicians in representative interest groups is due to the nature of the party political struggle. As yet the sphere that is appropriate to party political conflict has not been defined and limited, and all group activity is regarded in a party political light, with the consequence that, so far as party politicians are concerned, no organisation can safely be exempted from attention. Whatever the reasons, as soon as ministers in their capacity of party politicians seek to attach representative associations to themselves and to their party, these associations cease to be effective instruments for achieving the goals intended for them by administrators.

Yet the difficulty of maintaining a cooperative working relationship with suitable interest groups cannot be attributed only to the lack of balancing interests, or to party political circumstances; there is in addition the problem that the benefits the governments are able to offer are frequently inadequate. The level of expectations in this society is running way beyond what the governments can satisfy. Consider the demands of the town progressive unions in the Western Region. Every union demands for its town a post office, electricity supplies, tarred approach roads, water supplies, government supported industries; the larger ones demand their own hospitals and so on. Yet the government is able to meet only a small number of these requests. In such circumstances it is difficult for the Administration to maintain a smooth-working and harmonious relationship with progressive unions or with representative associations, and interest groups for their part have difficulty in maintaining, without coercion, the undivided support of members or of those in their towns.

These are four interrelated difficulties that arise in relations between interest groups and the Administration. There is one other on a personal level which civil servants have encountered in their attempts at cooperating with interest groups. Many civil servants are exposed to a personal contact with interest groups that brings with it a conflict between what is required of them as civil servants and what is expected of them as individual members of some other social group. As a civil servant a man is expected, as this Institute of Administration's code of ethics expresses it, 'to put loyalty to the highest moral principles above loyalty to persons, party or government department . . . never to discriminate by the dispensing of special favours or privileges to anyone . . .' Yet as the son of a particular town and the member of a particular family he is expected to favour the interests of that particular town or family. You will recall the career of Obi Okonkwo in Chinua Achebe's *No Longer At Ease*, and how part of Obi Okonkwo's difficulty arose from what was expected of the secretary to the Scholarship Board by the Umuofia Progressive Union, his messenger, Charles Ibe, the Mark family and others. External interest groups do not share with civil servants their belief in a common set of values, and they do not, in consequence, altogether recognise and respect the role of civil servant; alternatively, they expect an individual to give priority to his role of family member or son of a particular town over that of civil servant. Without recognition and acceptance of the role of civil servant and the values that attach to this, contact between certain interest groups and civil servants presents problems to the latter.

To some civil servants a solution to these difficulties is a cry, almost of despair, that all interest groups should be banished, and the civil service insulated from their activities. Were the government to narrow the scope of its activities, it would be possible to reduce the extent of necessary contact with interest groups; or, if the government had far greater resources of money and trained personnel, it could greatly expand the bureaucratic machine and bring the individual cocoa farmer or bicycle repairer under its immediate direction. But neither of these courses of action is practicable. Interest groups play a necessary part in government, both in policy formulation and in its administration.

There is no blanket solution to the difficulties that arise from the need for contact with interest groups: it is a matter of facing problems as they arise. Where there are no suitable interest groups in a particular area of administrative activity, it is necessary for the Administration to encourage them so that it is provided with a means of gathering information, of educating the relevant section of the public, and gaining compliance with government policy. It may, in addition, be advantageous to encourage new interest groups so as to counteract the overstrong influence of one particular group. It will be necessary also to use the powers available to the Administration to influence the behaviour of interest groups: the Administration controls the right of direct access, and with it the granting of information and a possible share in policy formulation; it determines the membership of formal advisory bodies, and is able to grant other favours; and for the exercise of these the Administration is able to demand reciprocal concessions from interest groups. The problem of how to prevent representative interest groups becoming involved in party politics is one for which a solution is less easy to see. To some extent the Administration is able to use its powers to discourage participation in party politics, but it is easier to take action to discourage contact with opposition parties than with ruling ones. The most, it seems, that can be said is that civil servants are in a position to educate ministers in the implication of overt attempts at the direct exploitation of interest groups for electoral purposes, and here civil servants could well be assisted by the widespread popular awareness that when an organisation becomes involved in party politics this generally dooms its non-party political activities. Finally, the variety of ways in which the problems arising from the personal demands made on civil servants can be dealt with is too big a subject to consider in this paper: it involves the whole question of how to eradicate corrupt practices, and it is concerned, therefore, not simply with how to enforce particular patterns of behaviour in the civil service, but with the establishment of agreed values in the society.

It is clear that interest groups are active in Nigeria. In this paper I have explained how they operate and how they are used. They constitute an important and necessary adjunct to the Administration. There are difficulties in this relationship, and these go beyond what is common in more industrialised societies: in Nigerian society, as no doubt in others where the government has comparable objectives and where the stage of industrial development is similar, there are particular circumstances that serve to complicate relations between the Administration and interest groups. To these difficulties there is no simple solution, but at least if the problems are recognised and faced, the Administration is that better equipped to seek to circumvent each particular problem as it arises.

5

The contribution of politicians and administrators to Nigeria's national economic planning

A. A. Ayida

This paper deals with the place of politics and administration in Nigeria's first attempt to formulate and execute a National Development Plan as seen by a senior civil servant. It is perhaps more interesting to talk about the role of the politician and the administrator in Nigeria's recent planning experience, particularly as the abrupt change of government on January 15th gives the Nigerian authorities a rare opportunity to reappraise their economic institutions and the public policies required for the efficient management of the Nigerian economy. In any reappraisal, knowledge of past mistakes, difficulties and achievements is relevant. It is, therefore, hoped that this paper will enhance the general knowledge of the working of the Nigerian economic system.

This is not a critique of the so-called past régime. It is admittedly easier to have the courage to criticise a 'dead' régime than to analyse critically the weaknesses in a current régime, particularly where the latter is a military democracy. What follows are in effect random jottings about what the politician and the administrator tried, or failed, to do in the field of national economic planning in the so-called first Republic.

It is too early to analyse the full impact of January 15th and subsequent events on the national administrative machinery. The impact on the politicians was felt immediately. With the establishment of the Military Government, the politician was dead. But the Nigerian establishment as such was not dismantled or dislodged. The establishment appeared only to have been shaken to the foundations.

It was relatively easy for the former federal and regional governments to draw up a National Development Plan 1962–8, however loosely integrated (if at all) the respective government development programmes were. But it required all the 55·6 million Nigerians to implement the National Development Plan. If they failed to do this, it was due partly to the national characteristics of the Nigerians themselves but more to the failings of the politician and the administrator. Getting the people involved in national planning must, in the final analysis, depend on the initiative and leadership of the politician and the economic administrator.

National development planning which involves the problems of implementation on the scale encountered in Nigeria's recent experiences consists of two elements, namely, investment targets and interrelated capital projects on the one hand, and a series of public policies on the other. The plan administration must be clear on the policies it will pursue in the various areas of social and economic activities during the plan period. On the projects side, economists tend to judge the efficacy of a national plan by applying consistency tests; whether one project complements another, and to what extent two or more projects are incompatible with one another, and so forth. They also talk about the viability and the social cost/benefit ratios of the individual projects. When economists are appraising the National Plan in the sense of projects plus public policies, they talk of completeness or comprehensive planning. Here there is some semantic difficulty, particularly when one recognises what one might call the ideological approach to economic planning. Socialists of most brands will not admit that a national plan is complete unless it covers every aspect of social and economic activities in the economy. On the other hand, if one adopts a more pragmatic approach the National Plan could be said to be complete if both the projects and the public policies built into the Plan cover the major activity areas in the economy. Thus on the latter showing, public capital development programmes do not have to cover every sector of activity before you have a national plan. It is most essential, however, that government policies should cover every major activity area in the economy through the plan period.

In the Nigerian context, national economic planning must have two fundamental objectives. It must lead to a rapid growth of the national economy and, of course, ensure optimum use of resources available to the economy. It must also lead to structural and institutional changes which will eventually sustain the development of the economy. There are other objectives such as an increase in the average standard of living and the alleviation of the unemployment problem. But these are *a priori* derivable from the growth objective in the proper social context.

When people talk of the failures of the current Six-year National Development Plan, they very often do not distinguish between the failures of the old régime and the failures of the National Plan as such. If it is agreed that the National Development Plan consists of a series of projects and a set of public policies, one can only meaningfully talk of the failures of the Plan by either pointing out inconsistencies in the policies, inadequacies of the policy prescriptions or failures of some of the policies or some of the projects. It does not therefore, make sense to talk of the failures of all the projects. The failures of the policies or projects could also imply defects in the way these are implemented. It is rather late in the day to try to appraise the current Plan in global terms. It will be more fruitful to consider the problems of plan implementation under the first Republic and in the new Nigeria.

Before coming to the administrative and technical obstacles to rational planning decisions in the former set-up, it might be preferable to dispose of some of the political and general bottlenecks which impeded the maintenance of national plan priorities. There were the traditional conflicts between national and group interests. But in Nigeria the latter were conspicuously entrenched in the political process, particularly in the regional-tribal nexus and sectionalised political party rivalry. The major political obstacle to the maintenance of national plan priorities in Nigeria was and remains what might be called the inordinate ambition of the major tribal groups seemingly coterminous with the former regional groupings. There were three of them under the old régime and, as long as the tripod theory of power in Nigeria subsisted, the unhealthy rivalry among the three major groupings made rational plan administration in Lagos impossible.

There was the classic example of the location problem of the Iron and Steel complex, recently described as the symbol of national disunity in the first National Development Plan. The former federal government and the three former regional governments included an Iron and Steel complex in their respective development programmes reproduced in the National Development Plan 1962–8 document as approved by the National Economic Council. The location question was shelved until the project feasibility study was completed in the course of implementing the Plan. The inclusion in the respective regional programmes was to ensure that the interests of the region concerned were taken into full account before the location was determined. In fairness to the planners, the project was not sufficiently articulated for the location question to be resolved before the Plan was finalised. When the National Economic Council eventually came to grips with detailed planning and investment decisions on the project, the politicians were naturally divided on regional lines. Some of the administrators ceased to be faceless technocrats, and their regions of origin either influenced their views or seemed to determine their expertise. Even the non-Nigerian advisers were regarded as committed to one group or the other. The intervention of the new Mid-West government to house the project did not provide a Daniel solution. Out of the wrangling and embittered discussions emerged the famous decision of the National Economic Council to locate the one Iron and Steel complex in two places in the Northern and Eastern regions (presumably by splitting the project—such details did not matter in the finest hour of compromise). The press announcement emphasised that a third Iron and Steel project was to be sited in the Western region as soon as iron ore and other raw materials were discovered there. In such moments of national survival through the art of compromise, economic considerations did not seem to matter. Nigerians were assured that they would soon have three Iron and Steel projects, though on financial and economic grounds the Nigerian market was barely large enough to sustain one modest plant.

There must be political considerations in national planning decisions. Sectional interests are not necessarily incompatible with rational plan administration. But in Nigeria the major political parties only provided the ministerial leaders, since the party apparatus, without an articulated and coherent programme, made little or no impact on the plan administration. The only exception was probably the attempt by the governing party in the former Western region to impose a programme on the government in power in that region, and this was probably one of the causes of the historic Western crisis of 1962 with its adverse consequences on the implementation of that region's beautiful plan. Most ministers in office tended to rise above the party and to build up their own followership within the party through extensive 'patronage'.

The 'patronage' system had disastrous consequences for rational plan administration and the maintenance of plan priorities. The consequences of 'patronage and corruption' on national economic planning are far-reaching:

(1) There are the obvious moral problems and the inequitable distribution of income in a corrupt society.

(2) The 'feedback' and other effects caused by 'para-contract' additions to the cost of projects increase substantially the financial burden of a national plan.

(3) The priorities laid down in the National Plan are usually subjected to substantial 'distortions' since project selection and implementation and the timing of investment decisions depend on their rate of 'pay-off' for a few (permanent damage could be inflicted on the structure of the economy through the establishment of a relatively few ill-conceived projects of strategic importance to the growth of the economy).

(4) Bad foreign private investment will tend to outbid and drive away the genuinely honest and the efficient, thereby contributing to the maldistribution of investment resources from all sources.

(5) The inefficient and incompetent administrator and the officials who offer the least resistance are often preferred, and

the unscrupulous flatterer or accomplice tends to occupy, or exercise effectively the powers of, strategic positions within the plan administration.

In such a system rational planning decisions tend to be negated or set aside at every turn of the road. New projects are introduced overnight without adequate appraisal. The concept of optimum use of available resources over the plan period is rendered useless. Planning discipline is lacking.

It is difficult to quantify the effects of 'patronage' on the Six-year Development Plan. All the visible evidence is that the influence of patronage has been 'marginal' in the choice of projects and investment schemes. Most of the projects implemented in the Plan so far are among those the economic administrator would like to see off the ground. There can be no visible evidence for the 'non-contract additions' to such projects except where these can be traced to the bastardisation of the tendering procedures, as in the well-known case where a contract for a bridge was negotiated with the second highest bidder at £1·45 million when the sixth and lowest bid from a reputable and technically competent competitor was only £0·95 million. Such glaring disparities were rare and were usually associated with contractor finance[1] projects where the credit terms are also relevant in the evaluation of the bid. It is significant that the contractor finance negotiated deals hit the peak in the crucial election year of 1964.

The influence of patronage on the selection of projects may have been relatively marginal but in the timing of investment decisions it was crucial. The point is that the Six-year Plan was so large that one could always get a Plan project for any deal contemplated. Besides, the National Plan was not phased, and since there were no programmed annual capital expenditures, the planners left the politicians with a package deal, a paradise for smart operators. Every conceivable project was within the Plan allocation and could be contained within the 'balance unallocated to projects' (block

[1] A. A. Ayida, 'Contractor Finance and Supplier Credit in Economic Growth', *Nigerian Journal of Economic and Social Studies*, Vol. 7, No. 2, July 1965. See also NISER Reprint Series No. 18

allocations which were to enable ministries to develop their ideas into feasible projects before implementation). The structure of the Plan, and the project articulation within it, did not therefore enhance planning discipline either at the political or the administrative level. The Plan was thus the devil's bible for all. With the benefit of hindsight, however, the structure and size of the Plan only provided one of the catalysts, since the will to distort it was ever-present in high places.

What happened in 1961–2 was that the formulation of the National Development Plan was regarded as one exercise and its implementation another. As soon as the Plan was drawn up, most of the experts, especially the non-Nigerian advisers involved in its formulation, were disbanded. The Nigerian administrators and planners were also moved around. However complete plan documentation is, many crucial assumptions are left over for resolution at the implementation stage. It was therefore difficult to time properly the investment decisions in the Six-year Plan without reference to the principal authors. This element is the more important in a completely decentralised system. The degree of decentralisation of planning decisions in Nigeria can only be appreciated from a comprehensive analysis of the institutional arrangements and the national planning machinery in the first Republic.

The institutional arrangements in a federation are not known for their tidiness, elegance and clarity of purpose and, as a rule, they appear to the outsider to be over-complex, if not cumbersome. Viewed from within the system, one sees a clearer pattern than is apparent at first. Nigeria's national planning machinery in the first Republic fits into this traditional federal structure. The principal planning organisations are set out in the following Planning Organisations Charts: A—*National Planning Machinery*, and B—*The Economic Planning Unit*.

The supreme economic organ for national planning and the coordination of economic activities in the federation was vested in the National Economic Council. The Council derived its authority and pre-eminence from its membership rather than the formal powers assigned to it. With the Prime Minister of the federation

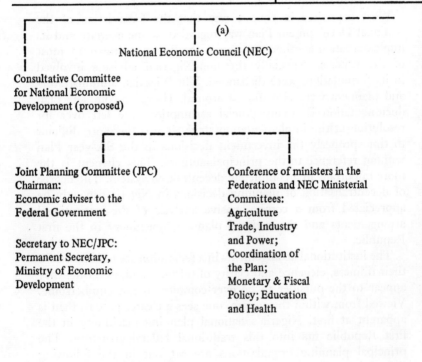

Prime Minister and Chairman NEC

(Inter-governmental machinery)

Link with Private Sector

(a)

National Economic Council (NEC)

Consultative Committee
for National Economic
Development (proposed)

Joint Planning Committee (JPC)
Chairman:
Economic adviser to the
Federal Government

Secretary to NEC/JPC:
Permanent Secretary,
Ministry of Economic
Development

Conference of ministers in the
Federation and NEC Ministerial
Committees:
Agriculture
Trade, Industry
and Power;
Coordination of
the Plan;
Monetary & Fiscal
Policy; Education
and Health

NOTE (i) Regional intra-governmental planning machineries are similar to the
Federal Government set-up with Premier and member of NEC as the
Head, and slight variations in membership and role of the Economic
Planning Committee.

(ii) (a) advisory and consultative
(b) executive responsibility

(Intra-governmental machinery)

(b)

Council of Ministers
(Sovereign body)

Economic Planning Committee

Minister of Econ. Development (Economic Planning Unit)	Minister of Finance	Cabinet Office Secretary to the Prime Minister,
Economic planning & development questions	Budgetary control	political and administrative authority;
Determination & maintenance of priorities	Annual capital budget, external finance	High-level manpower development and administrative postings
Formulation of National Plans	Fiscal & monetary policy	(Economic Adviser to the Federal Government)
Manpower planning and development	Resource mobilization	
Plan coordination; Annual development plans & targets		
External economic affairs		
External technical assistance		
Economic research on development Problems		
Statistics		

Ministers responsible for
executing ministries and
statutory agencies; major
sectoral planning units
and projects preparation
and implementation

c

Federal Ministry of Economic Development
Economic Planning Unit

Economic Planning Unit (EPU)	National Manpower Board	Technical Assistance Division
Chief Planning Officer (Permanent Secretary grade)	Secretary to the Board & Secretariat Manpower planning and coordination of manpower development policies; Manpower research and productivity studies	Coordination and processing of external technical assistance activities relating technical assistance to plan priorities
Agricultural planning; Development research priorities	Projects evaluation and analysis	Plan coordination; Annual plans and investment targets; Maintenance of plan objectives and priorities

NEC/JPC
secretariat

NOTE: Each section in the EPU is headed by a Senior Planning Officer (SAS Grade) assisted by Planning Officers (Principal Grade) and Assistant Planning Officers (Assistant Secretary Grade). Principal Planning Officers (Deputy Permanent Secretary Grade) may eventually supervise a group of sections or head such large divisions as projects evaluation with an authorized planning staff complement of ten (including seven vacancies!).

Permanent Secretary

Deputy Permanent Secretary

External Economic Relations Division	Nigerian Institute of Social and Economic Research	Federal Office of Statistics
External Economic affairs; Relations with international economic institutions; Economic commission for Africa; Chad Basin Commission; Niger Delta Development Board	Applied economic research on national development problems	Chief Statistician: Statistical data; Statistics, development and operations
Progress reports: Surveys of the economy; Sectoral analysis; Comparative planning	Resources: Monetary and fiscal affairs; External finance and plan priorities	Perspective planning: Balance of payments and other macro-projections forecasting trends in the economy

as chairman and the regional premiers and the most senior federal minister leading their respective government delegations, the Council was more than a consultative body. Though it had no power of decision, its conclusions were as good as government decisions. There was an unbroken tradition in the highly dignified atmosphere of the secret proceedings of the Council which enabled it to take decisions binding on the most reluctant government delegations. The Council could in a few hours dispose of intricate and politically explosive issues like the Binns' Fiscal Review Commission Report. On the other hand, the majestic presence and dignity of the Council proceedings did inhibit it from taking 'painful decisions' in the national interest. Where no compromises were possible or where such compromises were too costly in economic or political terms, the National Economic Council was likely to stall, however urgent the need for a decision. For a number of reasons, the Council could not meet frequently. There were occasions when it could not meet within twelve months. It could not, therefore, be the major institution for harmonising national economic policies, or for making day-to-day planning decisions. The federal nature of the Constitution itself did not envisage that a body like the National Economic Council would supersede the various cabinets, whether federal or regional. It was really the Council of Ministers in Lagos which was expected to act as the body with 'sovereign powers' over the major areas of economic activities. Somehow the Council of Ministers, from its very composition and from the fact that it depended on the political wills in the various regional capitals for its continued existence, could not provide the political leadership for national planning.

In national economic planning, there can be no substitute for inadequate political leadership. Administrative leadership, however competent, cannot rise above the quality of its political leadership.[1] It is in this context that Professors W. Arthur Lewis

[1]'Experience demonstrates that when a country's leaders in a stable government are strongly devoted to development, inadequacies of the particular type of plan in use or even the lack of any formal planning will not seriously impede the country's development. Conversely, in the absence of political commitments or stability, the most advanced form of planning will not make

and O. Aboyade refer to the crucial role of 'charismatic leadership'[1] in the development process. This is important in evaluating the efficacy of the national planning machinery in Nigeria. It is not often realised, however, that 'charismatic leadership' in the wrong direction can lead a nation's economy to ruin within a relatively short time.

There are ten basic elements to look for in a planned system of the type generally found in developing countries, and the adequacy of a national planning machinery really depends on the extent it satisfies or embraces the following criteria:

(1) *The will to plan* It is essential that at the national level there should be some collective wish for national planning and the coordination of economic activities so as to rationalise and optimise the use of the scarce resources available to the developing country concerned. It is now generally recognised that market forces alone and the existing market price structure in developing countries cannot generate a satisfactory rate of growth. There must therefore exist the will to plan and manage the economy at the national level, however decentralised the system.

(2) *Technical planning apparatus* There should be some technical apparatus for interpreting the statistical and other available data, and for marshalling the objective evidence required

a significant contribution towards development.' Albert Waterston, *Development Planning—Lessons of Experience*. Johns Hopkins Press, 1965. [1]'If a community is fortunate to have a good leader born at a crucial time in its history, who catches the imagination of his people and guides them through a formative experience, he will create traditions and legends and standards which weave themselves into the thinking of his people and govern their behaviour through many centuries. . . .' W. Arthur Lewis, *The Theory of Economic Growth*. R. D. Irwin, Homewood, Ill., 1955.
'The planner must all along be cautious that he does not attempt to supplant the community's preference function by invoking his own subjective conception of the social will. The risk of this happening is especially great in an economy with a political power vacuum as opposed to one with a clear, positive, dynamic and charismatic leadership.' O. Aboyade, *Foundations of an African Economy: A study of Investment and Growth in Nigeria*. Praeger, 1966.

for the national planning and coordination of major investment decisions and the development expenditure patterns and policies needed for national development. The level of competence and the effectiveness of such an apparatus will depend to a large extent on the quality and the professional skills of the staff manning it. The Economic Planning Unit in the federal Ministry of Economic Development was to provide the central pivot in collaboration with the regional planning units.

(3) *Statistics* In developing countries, the statistical data available are notoriously scanty. Even where the data have been collected with no excessive time-lag, they are very often not in the digested form in which they can be easily assembled and used for rational economic decisions, which should as far as possible be based on verifiable data. There is therefore a need for an organisation responsible for the collation and systematic analysis of statistical data on the economy, as in the National Office of Statistics, Lagos.

(4) *Budgetary control mechanism* There must be an effective system of budgetary control and sanctions for relating aggregate expenditure to total resources available and for ensuring that executive ministries and organisations keep within approved plan allocations, targets and priorities. This is one of the main responsibilities of the federal Ministry of Finance assisted by the Economic Planning Unit in respect of development expenditure.

(5) *Foreign exchange budgeting* Foreign exchange is one of the major constraints in plan administration, and the rational use of foreign exchange resources is a *sine qua non* for rapid economic development. Machinery for the rational allocation of available foreign exchange resources is therefore essential. This may take the form of annual foreign exchange budgeting to meet the planned external payments requirements for the year. With a relatively liberal foreign exchange régime, the federal Ministry of Finance assisted by the Central Bank of

Nigeria maintains only 'policing' or fire-extinguisher operations.

(6) *Coordination of external aid* External financial aid and technical assistance should be organised in such a way as to reflect the priorities of and meet the development requirements of the recipient. There is therefore a great need for some machinery for coordinating and channelling all external financial and technical assistance to the development activities and priority projects in the recipient economy. The federal Ministries of Finance and Economic Development work together very closely in this field.

(7) *Research on development* Research on development questions should be properly organised to meet the requirements of national development planning. The emphasis should be on applied research for development, covering industrial, agricultural and economic research. Such research should however extend to sociological investigations and other social fields if the results are to provide full answers for all the basic questions in planning and the process of social change and economic transformation. The Nigerian Institute of Social and Economic Research at the University of Ibadan has developed into a national institute for applied economic research and collaborates with the other research institutes, including the Economic Development Institute at the University of Nigeria.

(8) *Application of science and technology to development* One of the key factors in the rapid development of a developing economy is the extent of application of science and modern technology to the exploitation and utilisation of the natural resources in the country. There must therefore be provision for the continuous application by adaptation, transplantation or innovation of modern technology to the development of the economy. This would imply general diffusion of scientific ideas in the community and a massive attempt to inculcate the scientific attitude and spread technical know-how among

the generality of the people. It is now fashionable to talk of the need to apply 'intermediate technology' to the development of countries like Nigeria, particularly in the field of agricultural production, where the most advanced technology in developed countries may not be applicable. The equipment for temperate agriculture may be quite unsuitable for tropical crops. The notion of 'intermediate technology'[1] reinforces the urgent need for an articulate machinery for the consistent and widespread application of science and technology to the development of the less developed countries.

(9) *Manpower budgeting and training* One of the ironies in plan administration in most developing countries is the frequency of the maldistribution and underutilisation of high-level manpower and managerial personnel in spite of its acute shortage and world-wide scarcity. The relatively few qualified

[1]See 'Industrialisation Through "Intermediate Technology" ' by E. E. Schumacher in *Industrialisation in Developing Countries* edited by R. Robinson, Cambridge University Overseas Studies Committee Conference Report, 1964, p. 91: 'The "intermediate technology" will not reject any, not even the most modern, devices, but it equally does not depend on them. It will use whatever is handy, insisting only on one thing: that the average equipment per workplace should not cost more than something of the order of £100. This is an average to be applied to every ordinary process of production, leaving out those special sectors which are irrevocably committed to the Western way of life. On the basis of this stipulation any competent engineering firm can get to work and design the appropriate implements and methods to convert (mainly) local materials into useful goods for (mainly) local use. The types of industry to be tackled immediately would be:

(a) every kind of consumers' goods industry, including building and building materials;
(b) agricultural implements;
(c) equipment for "intermediate technology" industries.

It is only when, so to say, the circle is closed, so that on the whole, the people are able to make their own tools and other equipment that genuine economic development can take place. In a healthy society which employs an appropriate technology the argument that unemployment cannot be conquered for want of capital could never be true, because there would always be the possibility of turning unused labour to the production of capital goods.'

personnel available are, oftener than not, allocated to jobs for which they are not trained, while others are overtrained for the job in hand. Quite frequently, at the intermediate level there is such grave shortage that the work is not done at all. There is therefore a great need for manpower planning, training and development to be integrated into the national development effort. Effective manpower deployment from manpower planning and training, particularly at the high and intermediate levels, would also help to improve, directly and indirectly, the unemployment situation. The National Manpower Board has prime responsibility for national coordination in this field.

(10) *Accessibility to political power* The focal points within the plan administration should have access or be in close proximity to the seat of political power. Physical proximity is not synonymous with and should not be confused with unfettered access. Political influence and power may be derived from proximity, but the significant element for effective plan administration is influence and authority derived from easy accessibility to the seat of political and sovereign power. In the Cabinet system of government, the Cabinet constitutes the seat of political power except where there is a dictatorial Prime Minister interested in development planning.

The Planning Organisations Chart A (National Planning Machinery) shows which agencies were responsible at the national level for the various functions listed. In a highly centralised system, all or most of the essential functions listed are vested in the National Planning Commission or Planning Secretariat in the office of the Head of Government, but in Nigeria such centralisation was unattainable under the first Republic. No agency was equipped to handle the problems of applying modern science and technology to the development of the Nigerian economy. However weak, there was the will to plan at all levels, and every leader of public opinion recognises the need to plan. The adequacies and shortcomings of the agencies and ministries listed in the organisation chart were primarily a function of the competence of the administrative and professional personnel in the relevant organisations.

Shortage of high-level manpower in practically every facet of the Nigerian economy has been one of the major impediments to the implementation of the Six-year Development Plan. The cardinal point is that several of the agencies listed in Charts A and B have functioned relatively satisfactorily under the right type of administrative leadership. The outstanding example is the Nigerian Institute of Social and Economic Research at the University of Ibadan which was revamped from a defunct body into a national institute for applied economic research in less than two years by its new director.

It would be invidious to try to assess from one's personal and intimate experiences the effectiveness of each of the agencies listed in the Planning Organisations Chart A. There are questions of personality involved. It is easy in theory to say that institutional arrangements are made and personalities should fit into these, but in practice it is not a question of whether institutions are made for men or men for institutions. The two act and react upon each other in a Newtonian fashion which cannot be ignored in effective plan administration. One cannot really evaluate the efficacy of the planning machinery in the first Republic without pronouncing on the principal actors. On this score one must await the verdict of history to get the right perspective. However, this paper would serve little or no purpose if one did not attempt a short-run evaluation of the system from within, in the context of the New Nigeria.

One is often asked, how much did the Nigerian civil servant contribute to the apparent stagnation and indecisiveness of the old régime? The civil servant as an adviser in the formulation of public policies, and as the main instrument for executing such policies, is one of the key elements in the development process. Historically, before the attainment of national independence in 1960, the Nigerian civil servant at the policy level was neither a Nigerian nor a servant, even if he was sometimes civil. The expatriate district commissioner or the administrator at headquarters was like Shelley's Ozymandias, master of all he surveyed:

'. . . king of kings,
Look on my works, ye mighty, and despair.'

After independence, however, the Nigerian civil servant became the servant of all and sundry. The departing expatriate senior servants contributed in a great way towards debasing the image of the top senior servant as the adviser and confidant in the decision-making process. They pampered the new Nigerian political master, but he gradually came to look on the disciplined civil servant as the major obstacle to his exercise of absolute power.

Many of the top Nigerian civil servants themselves were not equipped for their new role of advising the politician on the running of modern government, particularly in the context of national economic development. Many top Nigerian administrators, brought up in the traditions of the colonial civil service, were more interested in routine administration. Many of them did not have the vision required for the imaginative task of nation-building in many areas of governmental economic activities. There was, therefore, an administrative vacuum at various levels for purposes of plan administration. One is not thinking of lack of academic qualifications as such when referring to the inadequately equipped. Not all civil servants had the courage and moral fibre to present their advice objectively at all times. On the whole, however, the Nigerian civil service can boast of being one of the sections of the community made up mainly of men of integrity, who are dedicated to public service for its own sake. The non-political character of the Nigerian civil service, particularly at the national level, has been demonstrated from time to time. This has facilitated the conduct of government business in times of major national crisis. Such continuity is very important for development activities.

The main question in the context of the future planning and development of Nigeria is to determine the ideal relationship between the administrator and the politician. In the early days of ministerial government in Lagos, the late Alhaji Adegoke Adelabu, who was then Minister of Education, called for a piece of paper one morning and minuted to the effect: 'Permanent Secretary, the

Action Group has started free primary education in the West. The scheme is very bad. I want to start a good scheme of free primary education in Lagos. Study it and report. I am going on tour and when I come back in two weeks, I must advise Government to take a decision with all the full implications.' The officials were given sufficient time to work out the full implications of the proposal before the government took a decision. The administrator and other professional advisers should therefore be given the opportunity to tender honest advice before the politician takes the decision. What is important for Nigeria is that both the politician and the administrator should act in good faith in the public interest. The basic assumption here is that the few politicians who in the past did not care for disinterested, scientific and objective advice have gone for good. The second basic assumption is that all public officials, whether in government, statutory corporations or other branches of government activity, will be adequately equipped to discharge their responsibilities honestly and effectively. This can only be realised under the aegis of a 'good civil service'[1] of the type which must be built up before the dawn of a new Nigeria. If all

'[1]A good civil service is a crucial part of the infrastructure, since the quality of all other public services will depend upon the quality of the civil service. This is even more important in underdeveloped than in developed countries, because of the difference in the amount of private enterprise. Over and above the normal civil service functions of running the public service, plus the regulatory duties which the management of an economic system now always requires, there falls upon the civil servants of underdeveloped countries most of the task of discovering new natural resources, investigating how they can best be exploited, finding investors for large-scale enterprises, teaching small producers how to improve their methods, creating and operating an infrastructure, and instituting and executing a wide range of institutional reforms. A good civil service is thus even to some extent a prerequisite of rapid growth. In this respect the record of underdeveloped countries is poor; failure to establish systems of recruitment and promotion based on merit leads to inefficiency; failure to pay competitive salaries leads to corruption; and failure to delineate the respective roles of professional administrators and of party politicians leads to confused decision-making. Development planning is hardly practicable until a country has established a civil service capable of implementing plans.' W. Arthur Lewis, *Development Planning—The Essentials of Economic Policy*. Allen and Unwin, 1966.

the major statutory corporations and development agencies in Nigeria were efficiently managed and properly run, the Nigerian economy would have developed at a much faster rate.

On the economic front, the new Nigeria is not yet born. The current period of national reconstruction can provide the basis for transition to a new Nigeria if and only if all Nigerians in positions of public trust exercise their power and influence for the public good—'Only he deserves power who every day justifies it.'[1]

[1]W. H. Auden and Leif Sjoberg, *Markings from the Diaries of Dag Hammarskjoeld*, Faber and Faber, 1964.

Part III

Civil service politics

6

Administration in our public services: a professional officer speaks up on bureaucracy

T. M. Aluko

I have not had the opportunity of finding out the exact definition of the professional officer. Do we have in mind the gentleman who has gone through a college education topped up with some two years' experience in the practice of a particular profession? Such a definition would include doctors, engineers, lawyers, surveyors and a whole multitude of other groups. But would the gentleman who has had a regular course in administration not come within this same definition also? You know; I don't. But I have a vague recollection that in my civil service days administrative officers were not classified as professional officers. While I know that doctors and surveyors, economists and lawyers together with engineers, architects and town planners are professional officers, I know so little of the work of the learned professions that I shall confine myself in these observations to my own profession of roadmaking, that is, engineering, and the allied professions of carpentry and masonry, that is architecture and town planning. I think I have some qualification to roam about the fields of all three professions.

May I, in passing, draw attention to the very important role that engineers, architects and town planners must of necessity play in a developing country like Nigeria? This, of course, is not to underrate the importance of doctors and education officers and lawyers. I do not want to be drawn into the fierce battle of inter-professional rivalries. No doubt this country needs many more men and women of all the professions. But it seems to me that the relative importance of each of these professions must be related to the need of the community for such men and women at the particular time under consideration, with of course reasonable foresight for the future. In this respect it is my view that at a period in the history of a nation when it is prosecuting a development programme primarily aimed at increasing the national income and the standard of living of the people, the importance of the planning, designing, and constructing of the infra-structure —the roads, water supplies, electricity etc. without which there can be no improvement in our transportation system, no expansion in our industries—cannot be over-emphasised. The importance of these is so great that the men charged with responsibility for them require special attention. Relative to Nigeria's present requirements, the numbers available are woefully inadequate. The approved establishment for engineers and architects in the Ministry of Works and Transport is very much below the minimum for efficiency and economy—that may sound like a conflicting statement but it is true. In that ministry the actual strength in the engineering grades is now below 50 per cent of approved establishment. I do not presume to know the accepted objectives of administration as defined in the textbooks on the subject. I should imagine, however, that these objectives in any organisation would include machinery for prosecuting the business of the organisation in a manner calculated to bring maximum efficiency and returns to the principals, be they the directors of a company or the elected representatives of a community; the establishment of an orderly, smooth relationship between the individuals in a department and between the departments involved in the whole administration of the organisation; and in the case of the public service a means of ensuring to the government, loyalty, and to the public, efficiency. But we must here lay emphasis on one very important point. Administration is a means to an end, not an end in itself. Administration in the public service must be considered as a means to the end of better living conditions and the social well-being of the tax-payers.

I believe that the ends of administration have been the same since the beginning of truly representative government in our country. But the means of achieving these ends have undergone much change even in this relatively short period in our national history. We have gone from the relatively simple departmental system of the late forties to the somewhat complex ministerial system of today. In these changes the professional officer in the civil service has gradually diminished in stature and recognition. When in 1943 I entered the civil service as an engineer, the Director of Public Works was a member of the Legislative Council. He participated in the policy making of government; he stood up in the Council to explain and defend the policies of his department. We note here that in our administrative evolution, even in the colonial era, when the maintenance of peace and order was emphasised above the physical and economic development of the country, the professional officer held a higher status and had a better hearing than he does today, when the emphasis is on physical and economic development in which, quite obviously, the professional officers' services are in greater demand.

If the effect of administrative changes has been to reduce the status and effectiveness of the professional officer, I am convinced that this was not the intention of those responsible for the changes. I know as a matter of fact that the theory was propounded that so much was required of the professional officer, and there were so few of them available, that they must be allowed to devote all their time and energy to the actual practice of their profession. All administrative and clerical functions would be taken off their plates. These would be performed by administrative officers, executive officers, clerical officers and clerical assistants. Who would quarrel with the logic of this argument? While no doubt all concerned have been giving of their best, the result has in many cases been different from the intention of the authors of the theory. Without in any way meaning to underrate the loyalty and industry of the men of these classes who worked with me when I held the post of Controller of Works Services, I discovered that I myself simply had to perform a good number of the functions that these officers were supposed to have taken off my plate. I discovered that in the long run this was quicker and more satisfactory. My superintending engineers in the field told me that their experience was similar.

Quite obviously, in the administration of any organisation there must be a set of rules and regulations to establish uniformity in procedure and to give guidance in tackling difficult problems. I imagine that the General Orders, Financial Instructions and Public Service Commission Regulations have grown out of this idea of the need for a codified book or books of procedure and practice. Add to them the circulars of instructions from those ministries and departments, like the Treasury and the Premier's Office, that have through the evolution of our administrative system acquired superior powers above the other ministries and departments. The vast majority of the instructions, orders and regulations still remain as they were when first made, and today they take their place with the new circulars, the dead contaminating the living, in the administration of the public service.

What has always baffled me as a professional officer at the head of a ministry is, first, the difficulty of persuading my colleagues of the administrative class to see the need for burying or burning the dead as soon as we find that they are truly dead, and of appointing worthy successors in their place, successors that can adequately answer the needs of our 1966 administration. My next difficulty is the thousand and one hurdles that must be cleared before a change can be effected, even after those concerned have been convinced of the necessity for the change.

Administration, I must repeat, is a means to an end and not an end in itself. Any aspect of our administration which worships General Orders and Financial Instructions and Public Service Commission Regulations as if these rules and regulations are an end in themselves requires serious examination. I do not know the history of the promotion of the Treasury to the eminent position it now occupies relative to the other ministries and departments of government. I have an idea that this must be connected with a similar practice in the United Kingdom. Whatever that history is, when aspects of Treasury control produce the very opposite of economy and efficiency in actual practice, then, regardless of the data that may have been compounded together to arrive at the offending formula, common sense indicates, and the good of the public that we serve demands, that this particular aspect of Treasury control be examined very quickly and cut out of our system before it becomes an inoperable cancer.

Take our recruitment procedure. We have evolved a system for recruitment which involves our Public Service Commission, the Treasury and of course the ministry interested in a specific recruitment. In the Treasury alone there are two sections involved in the matter. They are connected by some complicated, ill-defined or ill-understood formula for procedure, compounded of the scheme of service, the approved establishment, the salary scale and the entry point on that scale. An engineer is really not afraid of formulae, and indeed most of the work of professional engineers in the lower and middle grades involves the application of formulae. However, it was the nightmare of my office as Controller of Works Services and Permanent Secretary to find that all concerned in the ministry, in the Treasury and in the Public Service Commission never agreed, certainly never understood together, the application of the formula for procedure.

My incoming mail testifies to this every day. Yesterday it was a letter from the recruitment section of the Treasury, wanting to know from us if we have obtained the permission of the other section of the same Treasury to fill the vacancy into which we are hoping to recruit Johnson. Today it is a letter from another section of the Treasury wanting to know the entry point for the candidate. Tomorrow it is a letter from the Public Service Commission wanting to know this or that—all information which no doubt it has a right to know. Of course, we too in the Ministry of Works are not idle in the matter. We fire back, shot for shot, in all directions—in the direction of the Treasury where unfortunately our bullet finds everyone save the person at whom we aimed it, and in the direction of the Public Service Commission— where we must of course couch our letters in well considered language lest we get summoned to the high presence, with consequences that could be embarrassing. And when we finally reach the point of asking Johnson to come for interview at the Public Service Commission, do we find Johnson? Johnson? Isn't that the chap who joined the Nigerian Ports Authority three months ago? Letter from the Public Service Commission to us:

'We have been advised by the London Office that the candidate, Mr Lucky Chap Johnson, has now joined the Nigerian Ports Authority. Will you now indicate whether or not you want the post to be re-advertised'? Do we want the post re-advertised? Yes, we do. For in the set procedure there is no other approved way of getting the vacancy filled. Then we start all over again, writing the letters forward and backward, going through all the processes again in respect of another candidate.

In 1961 we eventually reached the point of interviewing a candidate for the post of senior executive engineer. He was well qualified and suitable in all respects, and we said so at the interview at the Public Service Commission. This candidate was an Executive Engineer Grade I in the service of one of our sister regions. When he got back to his station after the interview his boss wanted to know why he wanted to leave their own regional service for the Western Nigeria service. He told him that in their own approved establishment there was no provision for a senior executive engineer in the particular section of the ministry, and therefore his prospects were better in the West. Then the boss acted swiftly. Before our letter of appointment reached the candidate, a post of Senior Executive Engineer had been created for that section of the ministry, and he had been promoted to the post.

It appears to me that, regardless of what the data were that were compounded into our recruitment procedure five or six years ago, when we have failed progressively to recruit the staff required for the services of our government we should review that procedure and devise a more effective way of getting the bodies we want. In 1964 the Training Officer prepared for me statistics and graphs which showed that, in spite of the expanding commitments of the Ministry of Works due to the Six-year Development Plan, we had steadily lost more professional engineers than we had recruited. What may not be apparent from the figures is the fact that the losses were comprised mostly of experienced engineers while the gains were mostly the younger and less experienced ones.

I was not fortunate enough to be in Ibadan during the exciting days of 1957 to 1960, when our dearly respected and most capable former Head of the Service, Chief Simeon Olaosebikan Adebo, was busy with his hardworking colleagues, planning the creation of an indigenous public service which actually came into being on October 1st 1960. We know now that that service was most efficient, to the credit of Chief Adebo and all concerned with it: it easily earned recognition as the most efficient public service, not only in Nigeria or indeed West Africa, but in all Africa. It has always been my feeling, however, that in attaining this achievement we have over-organised our administration beyond the point of efficiency. The example of the abortive recruitment of a senior executive engineer from the service of another region which I mentioned earlier is to my mind a case in point. Whereas it was possible, within the space of a few weeks, for my colleague in the sister region to get a new post created, the resulting vacancy approved for filling and a particular candidate of proven ability promoted to the post, the same exercise in our own set-up will take not less than a year.

I sometimes wonder whether over-organisation is due to the concentration of authority and functions in a particular post because we unconsciously think of some particularly outstanding incumbent of the post at a certain time. The sense of judgement and discretion of an able and experienced officer may today appear to justify the concentration of authority and functions which he may exercise and discharge well. But what happens when he leaves and is succeeded by someone of an entirely different calibre?

Again I confess that I do not know the history of Treasury control, but I feel that more powers have been concentrated in our Treasury than is good for efficient administration. The exercising of these powers has resulted in regulations and procedures which in a number of cases produce the very opposite of what we set out to achieve. We must not pay engineers and architects salaries higher than the scale approved in some distant past when the conditions were vastly different. Then, when we do not have the bodies to do the pre-planning and designing and construction work that must be done, we go to consultants who charge fees much higher than what we should have paid in salaries to engineers, even if we had agreed to pay the higher, market salaries. Because we did not have an engineer to fill a particular supervisory post on a very important water supply contract we decided that a higher technical officer in another station not very far away should supervise this contract. We knew that supervision would save the government hundreds of thousands of pounds on that contract. Then came the snag. The technical officer was entitled to an inferior scale of mileage allowance and must not exceed a certain maximum every month. The mileage allowance vote had practically dried up, in any case. Regardless of the fact that when the scale of allowances was decided no one foresaw this eventuality, we could not do the obvious thing, namely to pay the man another £6 a month or £72 a year, which might have saved the government perhaps £120,000 in that year.

May I at this stage say that my criticism is of systems and policies, and not of persons? I should like to pay tribute to individual heads of the Treasury, both in the finance and establishment divisions, and to the successive holders of the office of Secretary to the Public Service Commission in the five years and five months during which I was associated with them. I have always found that I have been able to achieve relatively much by developing good personal relations with these colleagues. I know that I achieved much more than my other colleagues achieved in similar circumstances. But policies and regulations that will not yield the desired results unless the senior officials at both ends are tuned to the same wave-length in their personal relations and in their likes and dislikes clearly require looking into. What is more, it does not speak well for an Administration when the Permanent Secretary at one end has to go to the Permanent Secretary at the other and introduce the currency of personal relations before any results are achieved. It is my view that it is one of the measures of the efficiency of an Administration that officers at lower levels than the top can get quick results from their own counterparts in other ministries and departments.

Treasury control which leaves the Treasury the final say, regardless of professional opinion and the data behind such opinion, has led not only to uneconomical economy, such as I have mentioned, but to ridiculous results in a number of cases. I have been told of a case where a ministry forwarded for approval the estimate for a new school. The estimate was above what the Treasury thought was reasonable or considered that the government could afford. So the officer in charge of the exercise scanned the various items in the break-down of the estimate; dormitories, classrooms, laboratories, Principal's house etc. I believe that in the depth of his wisdom he decided to cut out the classrooms. The setting aside of professional opinion has led to embarrassing results. I have heard of a decision to build a hospital for a given sum of money which was below the considered estimate of the Ministry of Works and Transport. It was decided to go ahead with the construction, leaving out the one or two buildings for which money was not immediately available. Then the day came when a most exalted dignitary went on an inspection of the work, then thought to be nearing completion, to the delight of everyone—everyone with the exception of the medical staff. He expressed delight at all he saw. Then it occurred to him that there was something he had not seen which he knew was a dominant feature of all hospitals. 'Where is the operating theatre?' he asked. 'Operating theatre? Oh dear, that has been cut out of the present programme, for reasons of economy.' The decision to leave out the operating theatre, I understand, was taken by the townspeople, no doubt through their political leaders. Needless to say, the Treasury produced the money for the operating theatre immediately after.

The results of non-professional men exercising their right of decision against professional opinion vary over a wide range. The whole thing may not go beyond the ordinary irritation which any normal human being may feel when he sees people doing the wrong thing, the consequences of which may not be very serious. It may be the silent, justifiable resentment of the Principal Medical Officer when the consequences of inadequate drugs in his hospital are blamed on him, or the frustration of the professionally qualified and experienced engineer when he is accused of lack of knowledge of how to build good roads when indeed the opportunity to design and build good roads is just what he is aching for. The Superintending Engineer can and has had to take in his stride the criticism of the expensiveness of Ministry of Works direct labour constructions, even when he knows that most of this is due to his being forced to use old, inefficient, and expensive personnel who would have been retired were he not subjected to pressure from above to hold on to them.

When, however, the consequences of the decision of non-professional officers—be they administrative officers or politicians —to set aside professional advice affect professional standards, then it is not only the right but also the duty of the professional officer, both to himself and his profession and consequently to the public he serves, to raise his voice within constitutional limits. Standards that ensure quality and integrity in the profession must be preserved.

I believe that the White Paper on Integration recognises the conflicts that could arise and therefore attempts to define the relationships between the Minister, the Permanent Secretary and the Professional Head in the so-called professional ministries. I do not now have access to the White Paper but I believe that it is stated somewhere in it that the Permanent Secretary will not lightly set aside the advice of the Professional Head in purely technical matters, and when he has to set aside such advice he has a duty to let the Minister know what the professional advice is. I have for five years and five months been either one or two of the legs of this tripod in the Ministry of Works and Transport. In all that time I have seen the various aspects of the problems that could arise. I maintained excellent relations with my Permanent Secretary when I had—and I did have—a good one. I maintained fairly good working relations with another Permanent Secretary whom I considered not so good. He, no doubt, thought that I was useless. Then for two and a half years I was my own Permanent Secretary, with no-one between me and my Minister. I therefore had the opportunity of seeing both sides of the controversial question of whether or not a professional officer should head a professional ministry. I do not want to join one side or the other in the fight. I will however say this, that when I combined the two posts I had more satisfaction personally. I had quick results. I heard that outsiders thought we did well in the ministry—if indeed anyone can ever say anything good of the Ministry of

Works anywhere. But I am not going to rationalise from my experience or the experience of anyone else. For to do so would be to commit the error which I have criticised in our administration throughout. When we begin to devote valuable time and energy to discussing whether or not all ministries should be headed by administrative officers, and whether professional ministries should not be headed by professional officers, we begin to lose sight of the fact that administration is not an end in itself but only a means to an end, the end of promoting the well-being of the community we serve. Administrative theories which lead to excessive bureaucracy lead us further and further away from the desired ends. It was Dr Charles Hill, a former Conservative Minister of State in Britain, who once said: 'Red tape strangled the civilisations of Byzantium and Mandarin China. Bureaucracy thrives on delays and complications. We need to make our procedures quicker and simpler.'

7

Bureaucratic 'politics' in Nigeria—the problems of inter-class and inter-departmental conflict in the public services—a symposium

Chairman
James O'Connell

Speakers
F. A. Ajayi
S. O. Asabia
T. M. Aluko

CHAIRMAN Our topic is bureaucratic politics and the problems that arise in the civil service between one class and another and between one department and another. What many people think about the relationship between the senior members of the civil service and the politicians is that the politicians do too little work and the senior civil servants far too much. We have men here this evening who are isolated from politics and who make their decisions by rational and universalist criteria and who consequently are immune from the forms of thinking and ways of acting that beset politicians. Each of our speakers will make a short preliminary statement on this general topic and then toss the discussion from one to the other.

ASABIA For some time now, I have been concerned to find a satisfactory answer to some of the types of friction that do develop between professional people and the administrative class. We call this 'service politics', and I know that the suspicion and the resistance have their basis in a number of events or experiences in the past. We need to develop the cooperative spirit at all levels and the degree of understanding that is required to get our work done. I must say that, in our own way, we usually muddle through. Sometimes there is a difficulty which we can personally resolve, sometimes the problem is a lack of appreciation on the part of a member of the administrative class, and sometimes it is lack of communication. We should think about finding a lasting solution to this problem.

ALUKO   I have expressed the view (in the preceding chapter) that, if indeed there is any tension, this may be traced to the professional men who are supposed to have been relieved of certain administrative duties. These men have discovered that, instead of these duties having been taken off their plate, their work has actually been made more complicated in the process. The view that I have always taken in the past as a professional person is that, although it is not the fault of so-and-so in the Treasury, it is the fault of the system—a system which in 1956 or 1960 perhaps worked fairly well. Why have we not in 1966 seen the red light and the need for a change?

AJAYI   Politics among bureaucrats is the struggle for power, for territories, for spheres of influence or for supremacy. However ideal the system may be on paper, one cannot discount to any extent the personal element. The sector of this struggle that I have seen in my own short time in the service can be traced to a very large extent to the question of incompatible personalities. If you have a Permanent Secretary and a very senior officer next door and the two of them are agreeable persons, they will get along; but if one is truculent and the other is aggressive you find friction.

There is much that is wrong with the system. It is not very edifying for a man who is professional head of a division to find that things to do with his personal affairs, his leave papers and things like that, are handled by an Assistant Secretary. The tendency is to say, 'Well, after all, this man is very junior. Why should he be able to order me around, why should he push me about? After all, I am the Chief Mechanical Engineer of the Western region, and he is only an Assistant Secretary, and there are plenty of them.' I have seen this sort of attitude actually developing into near-fisticuffs in the corridors of the Ministry of Justice. When you have the arrogant administrative officer who does not want to recognise the limits of his own authority, this sort of situation develops.

There are areas where authority is not allocated at all. Occasionally someone will ask our ministry, 'Who has to do with the law of apportionment?' We might find that there has been no assignment of responsibility for this particular law. If you have an ambitious minister who is prepared to trespass as far as he can, he steps in and says, 'I want this done; I want that done.' If his permanent secretary will not try to tell him that it is outside his domain, he may tread on the corns of other people. I am talking now not only about inter-class conflicts between professionals and administrators but about inter-departmental conflicts. These things are avoided in other places by a sort of comprehensive arrangement whereby everything that needs to be allocated is allocated to somebody. We haven't reached that stage here in the West or anywhere in Nigeria.

We still have much to do to really improve our own system, quite apart from the question of personal relations. We have heard of human relations in industry, and I wonder if someone should not develop a workshop on human relations in the administrative class and in the professional classes. I think we could really do with it.

CHAIRMAN Mr Asabia has posed principally the problem of cooperation between the administrators and professionals. Mr Aluko complained largely about the system, and didn't mention his main centre of grievance which is the Treasury. In fact, he thinks that the men are constrained within the system. Dr Ajayi added the explanation that, whatever the faults of the system, they are sometimes worsened by personalities, and went on to discuss the problem of poor demarcation of areas of influence which tends to aggravate the problem of the struggle for power.

Now to direct the discussion to a specific problem. Mr Aluko complained that one problem was that sometimes one had to get around the system by using one's personal relations, and said that we shouldn't have to do that. I think that an administrator could easily reflect that no system is ever perfect, that if everything were perfectly demarcated, one would be in a strait-jacket. I should like to put it to them that, in fact, a great deal of reconciliation for administrators and professionals and even departments would be possible if one could temper the system by the good relations and the common sense of the individuals who operate it.

ASABIA   That is a very valid point. I don't know that it is possible to operate any system without having some regard for the personalities involved. Even in the best system in the world this element of the personal approach will always come in. I think one of the problems is that some administrative officers are so hopelessly incompetent that the professional cannot hope to respect them. On the other side, I have heard it said that it is because some professionals lack self-respect that they want to trespass into territories which do not belong to them. If they are true professionals, they should be satisfied with being just a doctor or a lawyer or an engineer and leave what appears to be administrative work to people who know more about it. They think administrative officers are the people who are supposed to know about such things as personnel management, transfer of staff and so on. People very often mistake this for the essence of administration, and I think this is part of the problem. There are more important things to administration than this, and it is the policy areas that I consider the justification for the existence of the administrative class. One possible solution is to throw the administrative class open to anybody who appears to have a flair for administration.

Another problem is the degree of competence of our administrative officers. The trouble starts when you have an administrative officer working with a professional who is several years his senior and who knows a great deal more about administration and especially technical administration.

Another problem is the sense of career in the professional classes. A number of people who are professional officers today might very easily, fifteen or twenty years ago, have joined the administrative class if they had had a chance to do so and if they had wanted to do so. I sometimes see signs that people are just not satisfied with their profession and the demands it makes, and get involved in other areas which, strictly speaking, don't belong to professional people.

AJAYI   What Mr Asabia said is true, but I have also known of administrators who are not satisfied with the field of administration and would like to dabble in professional matters. I have seen it in many instances. Some administrators are trained in law; and when in the Ministry of Trade or the Ministry of Lands and Housing they have a problem before them, they are supposed to deal with it as administrators. Though they have legal knowledge, they are not supposed to be legal advisers to the ministry. I have known of instances of administrators saying, 'I think this is the law on the matter—you don't need to go to the Solicitor-General.' This question of not being satisfied with one's own area is not one-sided.

You never get an ideal system, but if everybody would try to work within the rules with some good sense, I think much of this friction between the two classes would be avoided. If the rule says one thing so clearly that, even when you give it a legal interpretation, it cannot extend to the case in hand, there is nothing anybody can do about it. On the other hand, when the rule is very old, and you feel that perhaps the reason behind it has departed, but that it could be given some sort of commonsense interpretation, if you do that, I do not think you will be doing something seriously wrong.

I think we could borrow from what happens in many other places. Take the Judicial Department for an example. We have a system there whereby matters concerning senior officers are dealt with at the level of the Chief Registrar, and matters to do with pure administration and junior officers are dealt with at the level of other junior officers in the department. It is administration divided into two, and I think it makes for good personal relationships in a department where you have professional and administrative men. If you can get such an arrangement, it will help make for good personal relations. I have such an arrangement in my own ministry for matters of leave and increments for lawyers. They are processed by administrative people, but the final decision doesn't rest with anybody but the man at the top who is a professional man himself. This is something which is not very common. I don't think it exists in the other big ministries like Agriculture or Works and Transport or Lands and Housing. I think that an arrangement of this sort, if it could be made, might eliminate much of the friction that we have between the two classes, especially over the authority of the junior person who begins to give instructions or to order more senior officers about simply because he belongs to a class to which they don't belong.

ALUKO On the question of personal relations, we can criticise a system which does not produce results quickly enough, and this is not condemning people. In my own experience I have discovered that developing good personal relations with my counterpart has always yielded good results, but a system which depends on those at the top being tuned to the same wave-length to get results is not good enough. It should be possible for people at a level lower than the top to be able to get results from their counterparts. Human beings are different. It may happen that today I have working with me a Permanent Secretary who will see things nearly exactly as I do; but tomorrow if we don't see things exactly the same way, there should be a system whereby, in spite of our differences of personal approach and understanding, we should be able to get good results.

If I am a typical professional officer, the reason I would do work that is not strictly engineering is not that I want to invade another man's field, namely administration in this case, but that I want to get from that field what the administrator has not been able to get for me. I do not know a professional officer who really wants to be an administrator for the sake of being an administrator, but he may want to take some administrative action so that his work as a professional will proceed satisfactorily.

To cite an example, a few years ago, the training officer in the Ministry of Works was an expatriate contract officer whose contract was renewable from tour to tour, and it was desirable that we should have a Nigerian. Now the schedule of duties of the training officer is such that he should be conversant with the training, discipline, duties and practice of engineering, if this is possible. It is desirable that he should know something about the qualifications required before a student is admitted to a University, the sort of subjects he takes there and so on. We could not find an administrative officer with this knowledge. I then said that perhaps we could get someone with a BSc, not necessarily in engineering, who would have done something not unrelated to what we were looking for. We couldn't get anyone. At that stage, I wasn't looking for anybody but an administrative officer.

We had a series of executive officers posted to us to carry out the duties of the training officer when the expatriate went on leave. We came to the conclusion that most of the work had to be done either by the Chief Civil Engineer or the Chief Architect or by myself. It then occurred to me, why don't we add the duties of a training officer to that of one of the engineers? This sounded horrible to my administrative officer colleagues, but the only reason I was given was that the post of training officer was a scheduled administrative officer post. We eventually succeeded in getting an administrative officer. The point is this: I discovered that an administrative officer takes some time to get experience in a new ministry, and as soon as he gets this experience they move him away because he has no prospects in that post. If he is to get on in the administrative class, he must move to some higher post. But an engineer in the Ministry of Works who adds this to his other duties has the prospect of going right to the top of the Ministry of Works.

CHAIRMAN Could I raise an issue from an American author, Lucian Pye, that is related to what Mr Asabia and Mr Aluko have said? Pye has made an interesting and somewhat sorrowful comment on politics in Burma. In discussing what happened in the Burma Civil Service after the British had left, he put things this way—the British had a system and, while they maintained the system, they never took it too seriously. Very often, in the evening, two middle-rank senior service officers met and had a glass of beer and raised business between them and then went back to the office the following morning and set the business going through the channels. Pye says that, when the Burmese took over, they took over the system but not the personal relations which are possible in a very small expatriate group in a foreign country. So this system was extremely difficult to manage once

D

you simply kept the system. Could this be applied to the system which the Nigerian civil servants took over from the British?

AJAYI I think you are absolutely right there. They were so few and working far away from home. They had their clubs, and might talk it out over a glass of beer at the club. In the morning they would make the usual motions under the rules, knowing very well what the answer was going to be. I think it is right to say that even now we do practise a bit of this. I certainly practise it. There are things that my junior officers have tried and tried to get sorted out, but each time they are bashing their heads against the general orders or financial instructions or something, and they don't make any headway. In the end they come to my desk and say, 'What do we do? We want this thing done, but the chap at the other end keeps saying it is against the rules.' In some instances we examine the rules and find that they could be interpreted either way, depending on your mood. Occasionally I have been able to speak to the man on the other side either at my own level or at a level just once removed from it. We might have met at a function the night before, which has happened many times. He will say, 'Oh, I didn't know about it', or 'They didn't represent it to me like that in the file. If you will send it back to me, I will see what I can do about it.' Then the thing is done; not for my personal advantage, but for the benefit of the service as a whole. Perhaps we don't practise this as much as in the days when the British were here. I certainly believe that good personal relationships can go a long way toward softening the sharp edges of the rules and making a very big contribution to efficiency in the public service as a whole.

CHAIRMAN Mr Aluko, you raised the point of the engineer you couldn't get appointed in time because someone else was able to offer him promotion faster than you could get him appointed. Now do you think that there was any way that you could have got round the procedure? Looking at it cold-bloodedly instead of in the heat of battle, do you think there was any way of getting round the procedures so as to speed up his appointment?

ALUKO I imagine it was possible. The case in point happened

about 1962. Perhaps since then I have developed my personal relationships. Perhaps if one had known where to go at that time it might have been possible to get this man faster. I admit that, during the last few years, the relations between me and the administrative people have improved greatly and things have been done faster than they would have been done if these relations had not improved. I think this would be true for other professional heads and their counterparts in the Public Service Commission.

AJAYI A thing like that could very well be the fault of a man in your position. If he is removed from the details of administration in his own ministry, this sort of problem could languish for six or nine months. The thing to do is to take it up yourself and find out what is the latest thing. I am sure that if one did that with any reasonable Permanent Secretary on the other end, he is bound to look into the problem and find a solution, and quickly too.

ASABIA Consultation with people at the highest possible level should not be necessary in order to get things done. Even at the top levels, you may get resistance because what you are asking for is outside the rules. The person you are dealing with cannot disregard the rules or go to his boss because his boss will say, 'What the hell do you think you are doing? Can't you read?' So he wouldn't try. He will just keep sending you his opinion as a straightforward answer. Of course, it might be that if you spoke to somebody a little more senior the interpretation might be slightly different, but this cannot always be the case.

There are instances where the Treasury is arbitrary so far as ministries are concerned. A ministry might write saying that they have four vacancies for engineers and that they also have the candidates. The Treasury says, 'No, you can't do it'. The ministry drafts a letter saying the roads are in bad repair and that they are short of engineers, but they don't get an answer from the Treasury because there is no real answer. There may be an engineer coming in next year, or they are unwilling to pay expatriation pay or some such reason that cannot be given as a short, straight answer. It thus appears unreasonable and arbitrary, and this is no answer for the man who is dealing with it.

CHAIRMAN   There is one small problem which, in a way, I think there is no answer to, but I think it does merit a little thought. Civil service or university establishments tend to grow, not so much in view of the functions that the whole body should fulfil, but rather in accordance with the dimensions that they already have; and, this is modified by the political ability of the heads of departments. Now and then there is the possibility of some forward thinking by somebody or some group of men, who are able to think through the function of a service and say, 'Look, that used to be important in times past, but the establishment there could be halved. That used to be important, but now this sphere is very much more important than it used to be; we have more industries, for example, we have a lot more schools; we must increase establishment here, establishment there, according to skills of that kind.' Now, I wonder, what are the prospects for this kind of exercise within the civil service? Admittedly, it is a continuing function that must go on in one way or another all the time, but there is a certain inertia, unless in fact there is a kind of a revival every now and then. I wonder what are the possibilities for this kind of technological fanning which would inevitably run right up against inter-departmental politics?

ALUKO   I would think that at a time like this, when we are having expansion in industry, we should look into one practice which we have had here for a number of years—having a large number of people forming committees and meeting every so often, rather than everybody really contributing to the problem at hand. It has been my experience that people who are not knowledgeable in the particular subject at hand merely increase the area of difficulty. One example that has struck me forcibly is the Niger Dam Authority. This is an important body, judging by the importance of the assignment, and there are only five members. In times gone by, I think an Authority like that would probably have had twenty members. In the same way, I think a thing like this can come into the civil service where you have a committee for dealing with this or that. You have the Permanent Secretaries on various committees. These Permanent Secretaries, who are overworked, send their senior assistant secretaries, and they in turn send their assistant secretaries, till it reaches a level where what is done really becomes inefficient and ineffective. So my own view is that the time perhaps is ripe and the atmosphere exists for us to try some bold experiments in getting fewer people to tackle certain assignments.

ASABIA We have in my ministry a team in the organisation and methods division. They are not very popular because they are the men who go around and say, 'You have too many clerks here. What are they doing?' There are institutions in the country, like the statutory corporations, which were established years ago on the theory that they would be competent if free from the rules of the civil service. It was thought that, as they were commercial organisations, if there were no conflicts they would be able to make profits. We have found that this just has not happened. What has happened is that there has been wide-scale empire building, and all kinds of people who would not otherwise be employed have been employed. The question now is whether we should not go back to try to distinguish those statutory bodies which are profit-making and those that are just there, and put the non-profit ones under Treasury establishment control. There are difficulties and problems, but I think a compromise is feasible.

AJAYI In 1958 there was something called the Integration Report. That was a major landmark in making arrangements for administrative purposes for this region. I have often heard it said that the time has come when there should be another serious look at the existing position. Quite frankly, I don't believe for one moment that the O. & M. division would be able to do this job effectively. As Mr Asabia said, they are not very much liked in other ministries. I think it would be a very good idea if we got up a team of people, maybe administrators and professional men in various fields, to look very seriously into the problems of the civil service. Perhaps we are working a system that is already half dead and which ought to be pruned carefully and in different ways. Perhaps we can strike a balance between the rigidity of the civil service and the licentiousness which has developed in the corporations, where there are no rules at all in many instances, and it is a question of 'everybody for himself and the devil take the hindmost'. I believe that we need something like that, and the present atmosphere is one that is very conducive to it. We have this period of reconstruction and re-examination of the fundamentals of many things that have been taken for granted over the years.

Part IV

Politics and administration in the public corporations

8

The politics and administration of public corporations in Nigeria

Bayo Kehinde

I think it is necessary for me to start by defining the limits beyond which I cannot go. The first of these limitations arises from the fact that the political situation in this country changed on January 15th this year—a fact which was not within our contemplation at the time these talks were planned—with the result that I have to limit myself to the period from October 1st 1960, when Nigeria attained her independence, to January 15th 1966, when the old order changed. The second limitation, which I am sure that as administrative officers you will appreciate, is the fact that by the nature of my employment I should neither take any part in politics nor publicise any matters of a confidential nature. Remember the slogan—'Keep our secret secret.' The effect of this is that I shall make no reference to any particular political parties or regions and draw all my examples from incidents or situations which are obvious. I do not think, however, that these limitations are such as to diminish the value of discussing this subject, and I intend to be as frank as possible in my analysis.

The establishment of public corporations is obviously a convenient method of dealing with particular problems of governmental administration. They are set up by an Act of Parliament and are an arm of government. They have the advantage over a department of government of not being bound by civil service red tape, and they often take major decisions by themselves within the scope of their powers, subject to certain safeguards in the national interest.

The introduction of public corporations in Nigeria as a method of administration is a relatively new development. It was, therefore, only natural that, in drafting the Acts constituting the Nigerian statutory corporations, reference was made to the constitutions of equivalent bodies in overseas countries which already had rich experience in such matters. As a result, there are some similarities between the constitutions of the Nigerian statutory corporations and their overseas counterparts.

Examples of these similarities can be found in the powers of the responsible ministers, such as:

(1) the power to appoint the chairman and members of the corporations;

(2) the power to issue directives to the corporations where it is considered in the public interest so to do;

(3) the power to ask for and be furnished with any information which they consider necessary concerning the affairs of the corporations.

There is also a duty on the corporations to furnish the responsible ministers with their annual reports and accounts and periodical returns.

These are by no means the only similarities that exist between the Acts setting up our statutory corporations and those of other countries like Britain, but I have made special mention of them in order to show that although all statutory corporations are intended to be insulated from politics they are, in practice, linked with politics through the powers usually vested in the responsible ministers.

I must, however, emphasise right away that no statutory corporation is expected to play politics—just as the civil service is not. The link between the administration of public corporations and politics is through the responsible ministers and is not always a formal one, nor is it the only link. To illustrate this point, you all can well imagine that, in addition to the issuing of directives to a corporation, the responsible minister may also offer advice or make requests or suggestions. Even though they are not of the status of formal directives and therefore not binding on the corporation, they are usually not ignored. This 'extra-statutory' influence exercised by ministers could be and usually is quite a vital link between the corporations and politics.

Other links with politics also exist in the fact that the affairs of any statutory corporation could form the subject of a question or debate in the legislature at the instance of any private member. Nothing stops a member of the legislature from asking any question regarding the administration of any statutory corporation. There is also nothing to stop a member from introducing a motion seeking to reduce the vote for a particular ministry by, say, one pound— merely to enable him to criticise a particular corporation or play politics with it. Apart from questions and motions, it must also be remembered that the audited annual accounts of each corporation are usually tabled before the House and are later critically examined and commented upon by a committee of the House—the Public Accounts Committee.

In all these respects, the position in Nigeria is very similar to what obtains in, say, Britain. However, between the two countries there are quite substantial differences in the laws setting up statutory corporations and in the way these laws have been applied, with the result that the Nigerian corporations have been more exposed to political influence than their British counterparts. For example, under the British Acts, directives issued by responsible ministers to statutory corporations are to be mentioned in the annual reports of the corporations concerned, except where the ministers think that it would be contrary to national interest or security so to do. This means, therefore, that if a British minister gives a directive to a corporation under him, a channel is provided whereby such a directive could be made public, and if necessary criticised, unless national interest or security is against doing so. Here, in Nigeria, the position is different. Corporations in their constituent Acts are not required to publish such directives, and under the circumstances it is quite possible for a good many indefensible directives to be issued and for politics to be introduced with impunity into the administration of statutory corporations.

Another difference between the British and the Nigerian corporations exists in the composition of the various boards. In Britain the appointments of board members are normally made on a 'functional' basis. For instance, in the British National Coal Board, the British Electricity Authority, and the Gas Council, the responsible minister has almost complete discretion and is only required to make the appointments from among persons 'appearing to him to be qualified as having had experience of, and having shown capacity in, industrial, commercial or financial matters, applied science and administration or the organisation of workers'. Qualification is therefore the main criterion by which persons are appointed to the boards of the British corporations.

Here in Nigeria the position is quite different. True enough, our statutes make provisions for some board members to be appointed on a functional basis. For instance, the Ports Act makes provision for a member to be appointed from among persons 'appearing to the minister to have had experience of, and shown ability in, organising workers'. A few other members are appointed on such a 'functional' basis, but then we are all aware that under the old régime you also needed to be a good boy of the political party in power before you could be appointed. This is, in fact, putting it mildly, because in the case of the regional corporations appointments to boards were almost entirely a matter of political party patronage; and qualifications, even though provided for in the Acts, was not the deciding factor. With the federal corporations I think I am right in saying that although the politics of persons appointed on a functional basis might have been taken into account it was not the main consideration. On the other hand, many of the members of the boards of federal corporations were appointed on a 'geographical' basis to represent regional governments. These regional representatives were in most cases purely and simply politicians and no more.

These are some of the ways in which the Acts and the men controlling the various governments have created room for politics in our corporations. I am not, however, necessarily criticising our Acts or our politicians for this. Britain, for instance, has two major nation-wide political parties and a unitary system of government. It also has an abundance of high-level manpower. Here in Nigeria, there were a number of regionally based political parties engaged in a fierce struggle for power at the centre. We also had a federal constitution with residual powers in the regions. It is needless to add that our high-level manpower had not become fully developed, and there appeared to be no wish on the part of politicians to utilise available resources. If the federal government had tried to set up boards on which the regions were not represented, bearing in mind the political situation I doubt if many Nigerians would have had any confidence in such boards. In an attempt to have 'balanced' boards, room was inevitably created for politics.

Now, having gone into the sources of political interference with our corporations, the question which I am sure you have at the back of your minds is, 'How far does this political interference really go in practice?' To my mind, the degree of political interference depends on the following factors:

(1) *The financial standing of each statutory corporation* No doubt you are all familiar with the popular and perhaps hackneyed saying, that 'He who pays the piper calls the tune.' True to this saying, a corporation that is financially viable may not have the responsible minister of the Cabinet or members of the legislature asking questions often. Happy is that corporation. On the other hand, any corporation that runs continually at a deficit, whether through its own fault or not, will find that its independence is thereby diminished since it has to lean on the government for financial support.

(2) *Degree of the country's political stability* Political instability in a country or part of a country usually affects the working of public corporations to a varying extent, depending on their duties and functions. Take for instance a broadcasting corporation. In times of political stability such a corporation would tend to be allowed almost a free hand in managing its own affairs as far as news dissemination is concerned. In times of unrest, however, the government concerned would normally intrude very much into the affairs of the corporation

in order to ensure that the 'right' type of information was transmitted; and what is right in such cases is usually what is favoured by the political party in power. Opposition parties in turn sometimes react to this interference by criticising the corporation in the legislature and in newspapers.

(3) *Effect of foreign policies* The decisions of any statutory corporation that does business at the international level will always be subject to the requirements of its country's foreign policies. For example, the Nigerian Airways Corporation cannot simply decide to fly one of its planes to South Africa, even if such a trip is justified from a purely business point of view. Nor can the Nigerian Ports Authority shorehandle cargoes in ships from South Africa. This, I must say, is international politics, but nevertheless it is politics as decided by the party in power.

(4) *Quality of board members* As already pointed out, the majority of board members are usually politicians. Most of them are appointed as a matter of political party patronage. In such circumstances, especially if they have no other means of livelihood, they tend to place politics before the interests of the corporations they serve. This usually takes the form of board members interesting themselves in the political aspects of little personal matters connected with day-to-day administration, instead of playing their true role of laying down broad policies.

I must say that the four factors or modes of political interference in statutory corporations vary in intensity from corporation to corporation. For instance, in the Nigerian Ports Authority, I have personally discovered that although room for introducing politics was created by appointments of members on a party patronage basis, apart from specific statutory appointments of certain representatives, the board had very little, if any, political influence or interference in the popular sense. Deliberations on the board are purely on what is good for the Nigerian Ports Authority and the whole country, and if any member attempted to introduce politics, he would at once be called to order and checked for it, even by his political colleagues. Appointments and promotions were (and still are) made by a selection board comprising members representing all shades of political opinion. I cannot say whether or not the same happens in other corporations. Also, the financial stability of the Nigerian Ports Authority is such that little or no room is given for parliamentary or other questions.

Recognising the need to define the relationship between the public corporations and the legislature, the federal government set up a committee to undertake an investigation, not only into this relationship, but also into that between the government and the public. The committee submitted its report to the federal government and in 1964 the federal government published a White Paper on it.[1]

In this sessional paper it is stated, 'Government has, therefore, decided that public corporations should continue to enjoy an appropriate measure of independence and not be subjected to direct government interference in their day-to-day activities', and it was therefore decided that serious consideration should be given to the reorganisation and re-orientation of public corporations so that the corporations could play a more constructive role both in planning and in influencing the development of the national economy.

The sessional paper recorded many decisions of the federal government and it is as interesting as it is encouraging to see that they decided, *inter alia*, that:

(1) 'the board of a public corporation, being a policy-making organ, should be composed of men of suitable educational qualifications, ability, experience and integrity, who need not primarily be selected on the basis of their political standing or affiliations';

(2) 'the board should have a mixed membership of government

[1]*Statement of Policy by the Government of the Federal Republic of Nigeria on the Relations between the Federal Public Corporations and the Legislature, the Government and the Public, and between the State-owned Companies and the Government*, Sessional Paper No. 7 (Federal Ministry of Information, Lagos, 1964)

officials and outside members of standing and experience in business or other public enterprise'.

On the relations between the chairman and the chief executive or general manager of a corporation, the sessional paper agrees that there is evidence that no proper line of demarcation is drawn in practice between the responsibilities of the chairman and those of the chief executive officer. The paper admits this lack is a 'weakness' which, 'has in many cases resulted in a conflict between the chief executive on the one hand and the chairman and members of the board on the other'. To correct the weakness, the federal government therefore decided, *inter alia*, that:

(1) the chairman of the board of a corporation should serve as a part-time, and not as a full-time, functionary of the corporation;

(2) the relative position of the chairman *vis-à-vis* the chief executive or general manager, including their respective spheres of responsibilities, should be adequately defined in the laws constituting the public corporations;

(3) the respective spheres of responsibility as between the board and the management should be defined in the laws constituting public corporations.

In conclusion, I am confident of a very bright future for statutory corporations and the country as a whole. We are of course all aware that the present federal military government has started on those lines, and it is to be hoped that the succeeding civil government will ensure that politics is absolutely divorced from statutory corporations.

9

The administration of public corporations and the political factors

Z. O. Okunoren

I would like to begin with a warning that I do not intend to treat you to an academic meal. Rather, I propose to pass on to you the impressions I have been able to gather on the subject under consideration by reason of my long association with corporations and their administration in the Western region of Nigeria. I would like to observe that the subject of this symposium is not of my own choosing. As a matter of fact, it is a topic I would least have wished to discuss, having regard both to my personal experience and the terrifying atmosphere prevailing at the time the invitation was extended to me. But, as you all are aware, there have been some reassuring happenings in the country of late which have calmed, if not banished, the fears of many a public officer and which may perhaps have influenced my acceptance of the invitation.

My method of approach will be to suggest to you what I consider the vital conditions of effective corporation administration and thereafter to show how these could be or have been disturbed by political interference or considerations. Public corporations are created by governments as one of their several instruments, either for implementing their social and developmental programmes or for supplying an essential service which by its very nature and the magnitude of the capital involved cannot be left to free enterprise. Most of the federal corporations, e.g. the Nigerian Ports Authority, the Electricity Corporation of Nigeria and the Nigerian Railways belong to the latter group, while the regional corporations fall within the former category. Whichever the type, they all have some specific objectives to realise. To achieve these objectives, assuming that necessary funds are available, I suggest three essential conditions must exist, namely:

(1) a competent and knowledgeable board of directors

(2) an effective organisation structure

(3) qualified and experienced management personnel.

Let us consider these conditions one by one in the order mentioned. First is a *competent and knowledgeable board of directors*. Two types of boards are distinguishable, namely, a 'policy board' and a 'functional board'. The former consists mainly or entirely of members without any executive responsibilities. The task of such a board is collectively to take decisions on the highest policy level and generally to supervise the work of the professional and administrative managers. A functional board consists mainly or entirely of members, each of whom has charge of some departments or aspects of the corporation's business.

Whichever the type of board, competence will depend on the quality of the members constituting it. What then should guide those responsible for appointing the directors? In the case of a policy board, the members to be chosen do not necessarily have to possess professional qualifications. What is desirable is that they should be men of unimpeachable honesty, of high intelligence and good general education, with a real devotion to the public service and to the cause of economic development, a marked capacity for committee work, some experience in the field of business management or public administration, and a good reputation in the communities from which they are drawn.

As for a 'functional board', each functional member must have specialised competence and experience which he can bring to bear on any policy discussions requiring collective approval, and is responsible for ensuring that such decisions are implemented in the particular area over which he has jurisdiction. Unlike the boards of the federal corporations, the boards in the Western region have functional members. It follows therefore that if, for instance, an Executive Director (Agriculture) is to be appointed for the Western Nigeria Development Corporation, the appointee should have specialised knowledge and experience in agriculture; otherwise, he will be unable to do the work for which he is appointed. If he has not the specialised knowledge but confines himself to policy control of a general nature, the situation may be tolerable. But if, as often happens, he interferes in day-to-day administration and goes over the heads of departmental managers to give instructions to subordinate personnel, the corporation's administration will inevitably suffer.

The question may then be asked which type of board is the more effective. This is largely a matter of opinion, and it seems there can be no categorical answer to the question. Much will depend on the circumstances of the country concerned, as well as the objectives set for any particular corporation. Having regard, however, to the shortage of specialised men, I suggest that a 'policy board' is the one suitable for most Nigerian public corporations under our present circumstances.

The second condition is effective *organisation structure*. This term has been variously defined by different people, but I have been much fascinated by the definition which describes it as a pattern of responsibilities, i.e. a framework within which and by means of which the process of management can be effectively carried out. The organisation structure of an enterprise or corporation is therefore the framework for carrying out the responsibilities of management, for the delegation of such responsibilities, for the coordination of activities or operations and for the motivation of members. It is clear from the definition that this framework will vary from enterprise to enterprise or from corporation to corporation, depending on the aims and objectives of the individual bodies. For the same reason, it is difficult to speak of a model or ideal organisation structure of universal application. However, observation shows that a pattern is common to many big enterprises or corporations, namely, a structure in which the board of directors is on top, followed by the general manager or chief executive, followed by departmental managers and lastly by their deputies and supporting staff. All the federal corporations adopt this structure. All the board members including the chairman are part-time directors with no executive functions. The general managers or chief executives are not politicians and are appropriately qualified technically or otherwise.

In the Western region, only three of the corporations, namely the Western Nigeria Government Broadcasting Corporation, the Western Nigeria Marketing Board and the Western Nigeria Agricultural Credit Corporation, can be said to have adopted a similar structure. The following points deserve notice. Before the Army take-over, although the chairman of the Western Nigeria Government Broadcasting Service was a part-time director, the managing director, who was the chief executive of the corporation, was a politician without any technical qualifications. In both the Marketing Board and the Agricultural Credit Corporation there was in each case a full-time executive chairman and, in addition, a general manager, which seems to be an unnecessary duplication of functions, at least so far as corporation administration in this country is concerned. In the context of our circumstances, I am of the view that the organisation structure of the federal corporations is the most suitable for the administration of big corporations in this country, as it appears to be the type which can effectively insulate the internal administration of the corporation from political interference, or at least reduce it to the barest minimum.

The third condition is *efficient management personnel*, used in a very broad sense to include all supporting staff. The responsibilities of the organisation having been defined and allocated, care should be taken to ensure that suitably qualified and experienced staff are appointed to carry out these responsibilities, as the success of any corporation depends a good deal on the quality of its personnel. To this end, the corporations must operate sound personnel policies, particularly in the areas of recruitment, promotion and firing. Such policies, obviously cannot accommodate nepotism and tribalism. The ideal procedure for the appointment or promotion of staff is for written applications to be invited and eligible candidates interviewed by independent panels made up of top executives of the corporation.

Their selection should be final in the case of junior staff, and subject to the formal approval of the general manager or the board of directors as the case may be as far as the senior staff are concerned.

Having briefly dealt with what I suggest are the *sine qua non* of effective corporation administration, we can proceed to see how these could be or have been affected by political interference or consideration. Let us take the first condition, a *competent and knowledgeable board of directors*. The laws creating the various corporations vest the responsible minister with the power to appoint the members or directors of the board. Ideally, he should be free to appoint qualified men from wherever they may be found, including men who are neutral politically or even men from a rival party, for the corporation will stand or fall on the quality and integrity of his appointees. Ideally, too, politicians should not be appointed, because, apart from the difficulty of resisting the temptation of regarding themselves as their constituency representatives, they are particularly subject to pressures which may lead them to advocate policies or induce decisions which may not be in the best interests of the corporation. In practice, however, the minister does not possess the freedom of selection which the law confers upon him, and in appointing members he has to accept unquestioningly the dictation of his party, which is not necessarily based on the merit and integrity of individual appointees. As a matter of fact, the appointments are based more on party considerations than on the interests of the corporations. The result was that the boards of directors in most, if not all, of the corporations in the country were manned by politicians who could not give the leadership and guidance so badly needed.

The matter was further complicated in 1957 when a functional element was introduced into the board of directors of the Western Nigeria Development Corporation. Two executive directors were appointed to take charge of agriculture and industry, the appointments being justified on the ground that a similar pattern had proved successful in British nationalised industries. The analogy, however, is very unsound because, in the case referred to, those who occupy similar positions in Britain are not only professionally qualified but possess the requisite experience. The two gentlemen appointed in 1957, although good in themselves, did not have the specialised knowledge and experience which this type of appointment demands. This, of course, made it impossible for them to carry out effectively the functions envisaged for them. Since then, executive directors have been appointed to all the corporations in the region with disastrous effects on corporation administration.

In a report prepared for the Western Nigeria Development Corporation in 1957 A. H. Hanson, then Reader in Public Administration at the University of Leeds, wrote as follows on this type of appointment:

> I state these things frankly, even at the risk of giving offence, because it seems to me that the board has embarked on an administrative experiment which is full of dangers, and that these dangers are likely to materialize if the rather unsound comparisons between the British nationalized industries and the reorganized Development Board are unthinkingly accepted.

Those of us who are familiar with the internal administration of the corporations in this region since the experiment started, particularly since 1961, will unhesitatingly agree that these dangers have actually crystallised. Before the Army take-over the executive directors had virtually emasculated the corporations' top executives, including the general managers, had interfered copiously in day-to-day administration and had, in consequence, left the rank and file of the staff badly frustrated. Unless the present disquieting trend is tackled with realism, a very sombre future awaits the corporations.

I must in fairness say that, during the early and later fifties, although the selection of part-time or executive directors was made from the ranks of the ruling party, genuine efforts were made to appoint really good men who to the best of their ability worked unstintingly for the progress of the corporation. The position, however, has changed since 1961, and one is left with the impression that in making these appointments, particularly those of the executive directors, merit seems completely and distressingly to have been thrown to the winds.

I would like to conclude this section by quoting from a report prepared by the Arthur D. Little Group in 1963 for the government of Western Nigeria which admirably sums up what I have so far said on this topic. Though the reference is specifically to the Western Nigeria Development Corporation, the general position described is very true of the other corporations in the West:

> The tight political control over the Western Nigeria Development Corporation is also evidenced by the fact that all members of the board of directors are politically appointed, and traditionally have been chosen for their political rather than their business or technical qualifications. Five of the directors play a particularly important role. The chairman has been chief executive officer of the corporation, and there is no doubt that for most of the corporation's existence he completely dominated the organization. Four of the other directors, called executive directors, occupy peculiar and powerful places in the corporation, for they serve as operating heads of the departments into which the organization is divided: the Agriculture department, the Industries department, the Engineering department, and the Accounting department. Despite the fact that these are highly specialized corporate units, whose work is very technical, the executive directors have not been men possessing the technical training or experience necessary to lead their departments. The corporation has thus had political directors in charge of the detailed work of engineering and accounting, of large-scale agricultural development, and of industrial finance, rather than engineers, accountants, and financial, industrial, or agricultural development specialists. This has undoubtedly resulted in superimposing political considerations in matters at a level where technical considerations should be paramount. In most cases, it appears that the engineers, accountants, and other specialists in the departments have had to work under the daily direction of department heads who lacked the technical qualifications for any level of professional work in the departments.

We now come to the next essential condition, an *effective*

organisation structure. This is something which appears to have very little attraction for the politicians, possibly because they cannot, by its nature, bend it to their interests or advantage. However, I can recall two instances of direct interference with the organisation structure of two corporations. Some time in 1963, under a so-called reorganisation, the politician directors of the Western Nigeria Development Corporation, without reference to the executive staff or the board, created a new post of Financial Adviser; then they pulled out a highly qualified chief accountant from his post to hold the new one, and had him replaced by one of his subordinates. In January this year an executive director of the Housing Corporation apparently became inspired and drew up a new organisation structure for the corporation. But in his proposed structure there was no provision for a chief engineer. One wonders how the work of the Housing Corporation could be carried out without a chief engineer. Fortunately his proposal was swept away by the Army take-over and never saw the light of day. These two examples apart, it is safe to say that the organisation structures of corporations are not likely to be interfered with for political considerations.

And now to the last condition, *efficient management personnel.* As indicated earlier in this address, this condition can be achieved only if sound personnel policies are operated by the corporations. These policies should be aimed not only at attracting men of the right calibre but also at retaining tried and tested staff in the interests of continuity and stability. This ideal has not been realised because the politician directors, particularly the executive directors, were unable to keep their hands off personnel administration. They claimed a right to determine not only those to be interviewed but also those to be selected. In the process, merit was set at nought and nepotism and mediocrity enthroned. As for staff promotions, the story was the same. Many industrious and conscientious staff were superseded by less competent colleagues who happened to be the favourites of the politician directors. There is hardly any corporation in the whole of the federation which can disclaim involvement in this type of irregularity, and I dare say that a régime such as this cannot but have a deleterious effect on the efficiency of corporation administration in the country.

An unhappy feature of corporation administration in the Western region (and I am not sure of the position elsewhere) was the ease with which staff were fired. If a director did not like the look of your face, you were likely to be on the way out. If you gave an honest policy opinion to your superior which he did not like, you might be branded a saboteur, and the chances were that you might receive a letter a few days later to the effect that, 'owing to reorganisation your services will no longer be required.' This reminds me of an incident which occurred during my days with a corporation. The chairman wanted some ten clerical officers employed who did not qualify for appointment according to the rules, and in spite of the fact that there was no establishment provision to accommodate his wish. The report of the Coker Commission of Enquiry was then very fresh in everyone's memory! To safeguard my position, as I thought, I minuted to him clearly explaining the establishment position and added that, if he still wanted the instruction carried out, he should give me a written directive. He became annoyed on receipt of the minute, accused me at board level of sabotage and charged me with self-love, observing that I wanted to establish my innocence in the event of an enquiry. What saved the situation was the understanding spirit of a director who pleaded my cause.

It has been suggested that the worst punishment civil servants could suffer for their honest expression of opinion was banishment to minor and less pleasant posts.[1] Corporation servants are on much weaker ground and their punishment may be, and has often been, unceremonious discharge from employment. From available evidence, it seems that the politician directors believe the corporations exist more to underpin their party interests than to foster economic and social progress. The likely consequential effect of their handling of personnel affairs in the corporations is that sooner or later the corporations would be denuded of qualified and experienced men.

[1]See Chapter 11

What then could save the situation? The way out, I imagine, is for every government in the federation to establish a 'Corporations Service Board' to do for the corporations what the Public Service Commission is doing for the public service. This body, if set up, would be able, *inter alia*, to:

(1) guarantee continuity of service for corporation staff;

(2) facilitate the recruitment and retention of competent employees;

(3) completely insulate personnel administration in the corporations from political influence or interference; and

(4) generate public confidence in corporation employment.

It is indeed my hope that before a civilian régime is reinstated a solid foundation will have been laid for really productive and efficient corporation administration in this country.

Part V

The role of administrators in the
political process

10

The role of the administrator in the Nigerian public services

S. O. Asabia

My task would be easier if it were possible to get up a precise and scientific definition of what the administrator is; we could then have proceeded without equivocation to define his role. However, he does not admit of such close definition, notwithstanding the great variety of propositions which learned authors have sought, so persistently, to foist on intelligent laymen. Practically all of us are administrators of some kind; we recognise the individual who is incapable of managing his own affairs as a misfit, and those who have completely lost the ability to administer themselves as idiots or madmen. The bishop of a diocese is an administrator, or ought to be one, and a competent housewife must be something of an administrator and manager of the household.

Turning now to the place of the administrator in public affairs, you might well ask, for instance, whether it is valid to look upon the district officer of colonial days as an administrator in the sense that the Clerk of the Lagos City Council claims to be one. It is possible that much of the confusion and misunderstanding in this regard arise from the misuse of words. The district officer in colonial days, who went by the general title of Administrative Officer, was essentially a political agent of the imperial power; his primary concern was with the maintenance of law and order, and it is significant, I think, that his counterpart entrusted with the exercise of precisely the same powers in other parts of West Africa and East Africa until recently went by the grand style and title of District Commissioner. But the classic example of this phenomenon exists today in the countries, such as Tibet, Libya, Ethiopia and a number of small countries in the Middle East, where the post of district officer or district commissioner in colonial territories is given its proper style and title, namely 'Governor'. I suspect that the choice of the title 'Governor' is not accidental but altogether purposeful, as it emphasises the role of the person for the time being holding this office, and his relationship with the public, his subjects. The significant point which I am trying to make here is that the source of the Governor's authority and the extent of his powers in this instance are seldom matters for examination or debate by his subjects.

It would be unfair to suggest that colonial administrators were unconscious of the need to proceed by rules and regulations, if only for the reason that they were concerned to maintain a healthy respect for law and order. As a matter of fact, one of the greatest contributions of colonial administrators among us has been the introduction and the maintenance by them of the concept of the rule of law and the establishment of a multitude of rules and regulations clearly set out to govern the conduct of public business which, for much of the time, were applied uniformly to all sections of the community. Under a representative system of government, however, an administrator in the public service is required to do far more than this; he is required to work under the special conditions enshrined in the laws and the constitution and to work and to behave as a true servant of the public. In this important respect, he differs markedly from most other administrators.

The duties and responsibilities of the administrator in the public service must be exercised within specific rules and regulations; every act is supposed to be an exercise of the powers of the State. For this reason, the administrator has a duty under a democratic system of government to proceed with fairness and equality to all in the application of the law. Otherwise, he will undermine the very principles upon which his powers are founded. I propose to return to this point later.

Evidently, one of the major tasks of the administrator in the public service is to look and plan far ahead; it is his responsibility to foresee the requirements of the machinery of administration adequate for the needs of the nation now and in the immediate future. In the area of policy formulation, he must show the skills and qualities required to manage and satisfy conflicting interests of all types with a view to providing the facilities for the fulfilment of the legitimate needs of the community. In his capacity as the principal policy adviser to the government, he has an obligation to tender advice and recommendations in the light of adequate knowledge. In doing so, he must seek to remove or avoid unnecessary obstacles and pitfalls that would otherwise get in the way of social and economic development.

Under the system inherited by Nigeria, the administrator is not expected to be an expert but rather an intelligent layman, and if he happens to be an expert in anything, the fact is usually ignored in the course of his duties. The advice which he tenders must be based on reasoned arguments supported by facts, and he is concerned to enrich the quality of judgement and decisions by the application of experience and broad perspectives. In his day-to-day work, the administrator, as the representative of government and State, has the burden of endeavouring to protect the government from the political and economic consequences of prejudice and ignorance. While he must be concerned to act in the best interest of the government, he must bear in mind his responsibilities to State and society—something much larger and more enduring than the government of the day. He is confronted day by day by issues which cannot but remind him of the fact that adherence to sound moral principles is just as essential to the conduct of public business as is loyalty to the government of the day. He must be prepared, as a matter of routine and in the course of duty, to suffer and endure great torment in consequence of the need to be practical and sagacious in assessing the strength of conflicting interests, and ultimately come down in his recommendation on the side of what is judged to be right and fair to the community as a whole. But the administrator is for ever conscious and frequently reminded of the danger of causing embarrassment to the government or fanning unrest in the community. In consequence, senior administrators are required to be skilful negotiators. Oddly enough, under a representative form of government, it is to the administrator that the government frequently turns for an accurate assessment and interpretation of public opinion and the securing of compromises that are intended to minimise disputes and ill-will. But let us bear in mind the important fact that, despite all appearances, the administrator is no more than an adviser: ultimate responsibility for policy decisions and the consequences which flow from them rests firmly with the government, or individual ministers where appropriate.

I have thus far said nothing about the importance of routine jobs in the management of public business. These, of course, are no less essential to effective administration than the other factors I have mentioned. Thus, the provision of secretarial service, familiarity with the multitude of rules and regulations, committee procedure, parliamentary procedure, the tricks of personnel management, etc., are all of some significance, and competence in them is attained after a period of training and experience.

Most unfortunately, many people, including practically all young and middle-grade administrative officers, erroneously look upon these as constituting the most important aspect of their duties. It is even more regrettable that this attitude persists in unexpected quarters to the detriment of efficiency. The extent to which it has permeated the thinking of highly placed officials is perhaps attested by the content of the examination prescribed for young administrative officers who seek to be confirmed in their appointments: a test paper in familiarity with the rules and regulations, General Orders, Financial Instructions, Public Service Commission Regulations, Principles of Law (English Legal System), etc. The impression one inevitably gathers is that competence in these routine procedures is proof that an individual who has served in the administrative class for some three years is good enough unless he happens to have committed a heinous crime or has been foolish enough to rub his superior officers up the wrong way; barring these, the public is, to all intents and purposes, stuck with him for life.

I have for some time toyed with the idea of looking into this particular problem with a view to securing assistance in devising an effective examination system for testing some of the more important qualities relevant to the effective discharge of the duties of an administrative officer in a new Nigeria, anxious and impatient for rapid social and economic development. It is clear that the General Orders, the Financial Instructions, and the great mass of Establishment and Finance Circulars, the Public Service Commission Regulations and the rest are merely static descriptions of procedural arrangements which give little indication of the kind of practical considerations which must influence the formulation of sound policies. Mere ability to administer the rules does not make an administrative officer, just as you do not necessarily produce competent administrative officers by giving them post-graduate training in an institute.

I do not, however, wish to leave you with the impression that familiarity with rules and regulations is superfluous to good administration. I am convinced that it is far more important for young administrators in the public service to seek to understand the philosophy behind the various rules and regulations which they are called upon to apply and interpret, but first, they must seek to understand the needs of the society which they are called upon to serve and must acquire the tools of knowledge and the right attitude of mind required for the successful prosecution of their task. I think it would be misleading in the extreme to deny the great influence of new ideas and techniques, all of which have had such profound effects on the process of administration, both public and private—personnel management, training surveys and techniques, organisation and methods practice, economic planning, labour administration, etc. In an age in which the governments of the federation, directly or indirectly, through the boards, statutory corporations and a host of industries, hold a substantial share in business and industry, it would be foolish to ignore the importance of a scientific approach to the requirements of public administration. The great involvement of government in economic activities suggests very strongly that a competent administrator should be reasonably familiar with such things as the functions of the money market, problems of investment, economic growth, automation, international politics, etc. There can be little doubt that it is one of the basic functions of the administrator in the public service today to provide and assemble the expert knowledge and guidance required for the purpose of reaching sound judgements on the all-important goal of creating a happy and prosperous community of citizens. For while his political master, when he has one, is for much of the time preoccupied with more exciting issues, the senior administrator must struggle with the problems of research and analysis essential to the establishment of a sound machinery of government geared to the rapid promotion of social and economic development.

I would like to say one final word about the responsibility of the civil servants in Nigeria and developing countries generally; we in Nigeria have had practical evidence of the crucial importance of the place of these men and women in our own country and elsewhere in the emerging countries. It has been shown time and again that it is to the civil service that the public ultimately turns for the provision of the basic necessities of life and the maintenance of law and order on occasions when politicians and statesmen are preoccupied with more urgent and pressing problems. It seems absolutely vital, therefore, that those of us who have the privilege of serving the nation in this way must cultivate and retain a keen sense of service. And while loyalty to persons and governments is essential to good administration, it must not be forgotten that loyalty to the State and to principles are of paramount importance, for it is only in this way that our nation can survive, develop and take its rightful place in the world at large.

nsibilities of the Nigerian senior
... servant in policy formulation

Joseph F. Maloney

Recent events in Nigeria have brought about a suspension of
politics as heretofore conducted. Nigeria is now in a period of
rule by the military, a period characterised by some hostility
towards the partisan politics and politicians of the immediate
past. If we accept some simplified definitions as working tools, we
still can discuss today the role of the 'politician' and the civil
service administrator in developing countries, while using the
Nigeria of today as the country of our prime concern and as an
example.

'Politics' is simply the manner in which policy is determined.
'Politicians' are individuals who serve in government in response
to the electorate as the instrument of the electorate for the specific
purpose of determining, maintaining and changing public policies.
'The electorate' acts through formal elections or through other
expressions of support or disapproval. Clearly the Nigerian
'electorate' expressed its approval and support for the new military
rulers immediately after the revolutionary events of January 1966.
For the purposes of this discussion we will use the term 'masters'
as including 'politicians' and those military rulers who have
assumed temporarily the policy-determination power formerly
exercised by the politicians. 'Administration' includes both
the manner in which established public policy is executed and
the manner in which possible changes in policy are explored
within the government for final determination by the masters.
'Administrators' are individuals who serve in government as the

expert servants of the public. They are under the direction of the masters in the execution of policies arrived at by the masters and in the preparation of possible policy changes for final determination by the masters.

To narrow and heighten the topic for this discussion, this paper will confine itself to the exploration of some of the differences in the roles and duties of senior civil servants in the policy-decision-making process in the United States and Nigeria. In my opinion, a very important but little understood part of policy-determination in developing countries today is precisely the roles and duties of the senior civil servants. For several years now, some senior civil servants have made it quite clear, in a proper and discreet way, that they wished more of their policy recommendations had been adopted by their masters. The number of military rulers now active in civil government is considerably less than the former number of political ministers. It will be interesting to see how courageous the senior civil servants will be, now that there are fewer intermediaries between themselves and the issuing of policy commands. Presumably, the new military rulers will be more receptive to proposals for reform and probably more inclined to assign the responsibilities for departmental policy decisions to Permanent Secretaries. During military rule some of the former distinctions between masters and servants may become blurred.

One sharp difference between Nigeria and the United States is the height in the hierarchical structure reached by career civil servants in Nigeria and the depth in the administrative structure reached by temporary political appointees in the United States. Permanent Secretaries, Under Secretaries, and Senior Assistant Secretaries are non-partisan career civil servants in Nigeria, but in the United States similar posts are frequently filled by highly partisan temporary appointees. In the United States cabinet members and senior administrative officials four and sometimes five or more levels down from the top of the departmental hierarchy are strictly personal appointees of the chief executive, drawn largely from his party associates. Without attempting to decide if either system is superior to the other, we shall find the consequences of this contrast are interesting.

Fundamentally, the main consequence is that the obligations of the senior civil servants in Nigeria are much greater than those of the most senior career civil servants in the United States. Since they go so much higher in the hierarchy, Nigerian senior civil servants are in positions of potentially greater influence and therefore of greater responsibility in the policy-decision-making process. This is even more so since the recent change to rule by the military. Now all the numerous ministers have been replaced in government by a much smaller number of military officers with much less experience in civil administration.

One of the oldest clichés in political science and public administration, long regarded as dead and buried, is the notion that there is a sharp difference between politics and administration, that these are separate worlds, and that the master and the senior civil servant have completely different and separate roles to play. In reality, in almost every society, administrators play a major role in the policy-decision process by supplying and analysing information, alternative courses of action and the consequences of alternatives. In the constitutional republic of the United States (as formerly in Nigeria) the elected public officials have the constitutional right to decide what the public policy is to be. Now in Nigeria no one contests the right of the military to finally decide public policy questions even though the military leadership may be looking forward to the day when it can return the exercise of this right to popularly elected officials. However, the policy-decision-making process includes much more than that final moment of judgement. Policies are not decided without some prior exploration of the feasibility of alternatives—even if the alternatives are limited to the two of 'acting' or 'non-acting'. The extent to which senior civil servants are consulted by the masters varies considerably from one policy problem area to another. The same variation exists in the United States as well. There is no hard and fast rule which can clearly and in a quantitative manner state the proportionate responsibility of the master and the senior civil servant in the entire decision making process. Clearly, the Nigerian civil servant should be of greater influence than his career counterpart in the United States.

In the United States, cabinet members and the highest departmental officials are personal appointees who have been selected because of their established partisan or personal loyalty to the elected chief executive, and possibly because of their individual interest and expertise in the subject area of the departments to which they are appointed. Responsible chief executives (Presidents, Governors and Mayors) more and more are requiring demonstrated competence on the part of such appointees in the subject areas of the departments. This competence is established by a record of previous political party activities in the subject area or some similar activity in private life. (If a career civil servant accepts such an appointment, he is automatically deprived of the protection of his 'career' status and may be dismissed at will.) If the subject matter of a particular department is very complex and important to the community, the chief executive may appoint an individual with a minimum record of partisan loyalty (or even an individual who is a nominal member of the opposition party), but with some record of sympathy with the chief executive's policy in the subject area, and outstanding competence as an expert in the subject area (e.g. private bankers as Treasury officials, or chartered accountants as Commissioners of Internal Revenue, or an attorney with a substantial private practice as an expert in tax law as the Chief Counsel of the Bureau of Internal Revenue), or simply as a heretofore non-partisan expert in administration of complex organisations (e.g. Robert MacNamara from the Ford Motor Company to the position of Secretary of Defence). When comparatively non-partisan experts receive such political appointments, the chief executive first determines that the appointed political administrator is at least sympathetic to the chief executive's policy leanings and to bringing the administration of the department into accord with the chief executive's broad policy preferences.

In Nigeria the former ministers have been replaced as the top departmental officials largely by their former subordinates—the permanent secretaries. Moreover, the number of military officers fully assigned to civil administration posts as regional governors, etc., is considerably smaller than the number of former ministers and corporation officials dismissed from government service. It appears that the military rulers as a group have had less experience in civil administration than the former ministers and that a wide gulf or communication problem might arise between the Nigerian military rulers and the top civil service administrators. In the United States department heads and the senior administrative officials are partisan appointees who frequently have had substantial and varied administrative experience and who associate with other party-appointed administrators and partisan political advisers of the chief executive as fellow-members of that warm fraternity of politicians—as comrades-in-arms from many a previous political war. Frequently partisan-appointed senior administrators at the federal level have previously been state governors and mayors of larger cities or other State administrative officials, with considerable experience in the theory and practice of both policy formulation and administration. Such senior administrative officials are both policy and party representatives of the chief executive in continuous dealings with each other and with members of legislatures. Therefore, there is little communication difficulty between the political advisers to the chief executive, department heads and higher administrative staff.

In Nigeria the non-partisan career civil servants have a near-monopoly of professional and practical experience in civil administration. The senior career civil servant who goes higher in the governing hierarchy in Nigeria than comparable civil servants in the United States ought, therefore, to play a more critical role in the policy-decision-making process. He has a great obligation to acquaint the nation's new rulers with the limitations of civil administration. Of course, the senior civil servant must not claim a right of final veto over policy decisions reserved to the military rulers, but the senior career civil servant must recognise that he must often play the role of a persuasive teacher in a continuous and intensive adult education programme, now with military rulers rather than politicians as his students. In Nigeria, unlike the United States, senior civil servants have a knowledge and an understanding of administration greater than most of their superiors in the hierarchical structure—a knowledge and understanding probably greater than that of the partisan politicians from whose ranks were drawn the cabinet ministers and clearly greater than that of the new military rulers.

When career administrators give negative advisory opinions about policy proposals because of their greater knowledge of administrative problems and limitations, extra care must be taken to prevent this from being regarded by the new masters as subtle opposition or as an expression of a naturally over-conservative bureaucratic negativism. More than in the United States, therefore, the senior career civil servants in Nigeria must take continuous care so that it is obvious that their exposition of the limitations of administration is clearly based upon realism and not upon latent opposition.

There is also a greater obligation on the part of Nigerian career senior civil servants to serve as interpreters and as balancing factors in the relationships between their new masters and their eventual successors. Almost every recent professional article or publication on the difficulties of economic development planning in Africa has emphasised that major limiting factors are the lack of sufficient administrative, organisational and entrepreneurial skills. The career senior civil servant, more than anyone else, should have a realistic awareness of the true capacities of his government's organisational structure, and he must advise and teach accordingly.

Nigerian civil servants should not retreat into a world of their own. They should force themselves, if necessary, to maintain continuous contact with the general public and the various sectors of the public, so as to maintain both balance and perspective. Civil servants must develop and maintain a sympathetic understanding of both the needs and desires of various social and community groups and the practical limits of governmental power. Civil servants should be trilingual—understanding the languages of the people and of the experts as well as of their fellow-administrators.

There are numerous examples in real life, in both the United Kingdom and the United States, of broker-translators of the type represented by Lewis Eliot in the novels of C. P. Snow. However,

Nigerian civil servants must be their own broker-translators, bridging the pressure world of their governmental masters and the administrative world of the civil servants. The civil servant should be creative in finding ways to make the implications of policy alternatives more understandable to the masters. He should be better acquainted with the possibilities and the limitations of governmental structure and organisation in carrying out old and new policies. He should know how to lead the masters more towards solid achievements in reality than towards over-ambitious goals that can only be dreams. He must know how to manage limited means so as to maximise achievement of basic objectives.

Because they have detailed knowledge and experience in the affairs of civil government, senior Nigerian career civil servants have the obligation to give advice in a two-fold aspect: upon request from their superiors, and whenever they think it might be helpful even if not requested by superiors or if not warmly welcomed by them. While the policy-decision-determining power is finally lodged with military rulers in Nigeria, the career civil servant has the obligation to participate actively in the policy-making process within government, right up to the point of final decision-taking. Indeed, many a Permanent Secretary will now be expected to assume the final responsibility for policy decisions formerly reserved for his minister.

Several kinds of courage may therefore be required of senior career civil servants. One is the courage to talk freely with colleagues so that 'official opinions' may develop as a guide for the masters. C. P. Snow gives an illustration of such a development of 'official opinion' in his most recent novel dealing with the relationships between British civil servants and politicians. Nigerian civil servants can find a strong expression of this duty to play an acting role in the decision-making process in the modern British civil service—supposedly the pattern on which the Nigerian civil service is basically formed. At least, Snow attributes this positive attitude to his senior civil servants of the present generation. Speaking of a young Permanent Secretary, he states:

In one respect, however, he differed from Rose. He did not

indulge in any hypocrisy of formality or protocol. It never occurred to him to pretend—as Rose had always pretended, and sometimes managed to believe—that he had no influence on events. It never occurred to him to chant that he was simply there to carry out the policy of his 'masters'. On the contrary, Douglas often found it both necessary and pleasant to produce his own.[1]

An official opinion need not be unanimous nor need it be developed without taking into consideration the limitations of the times. Civil servants should not hesitate to explore thoroughly with their colleagues the consequences of contemplated changes in policy or of failure to change established policies, to develop individual and official opinions, and to see to it that such opinions are made known to their masters. If the senior civil servants accept this as part of their obligations, then in time the masters will recognise the wisdom of at least considering such opinions, even though they are not obliged to adopt them as their own. Some former Nigerian ministers might still be masters if they had listened more attentively to the official opinions of many of their senior civil servants. It is not an easy matter to make an official but displeasing opinion known (as perhaps a matter of official if confidential record) while maintaining the confidence of one's superiors. Under all circumstances, the master should have confidence in the determination of the civil servants both to keep any difference of opinion 'within the family' and to administer whatever policy decisions have been adopted by the masters. Of course, the Nigerian civil servant must keep his advisory role within the government and not engage in policy disputes with the masters outside government, such as in the press or as participants in the partisan electioneering process.

In Nigeria, courage may be required. Every responsible person should perform his duties as best as he can, even when doing so makes him unpopular with his equals and superiors. Fortunately for civil servants, the worst punishment for having

[1] C. P. Snow, *Corridors of Power*, Macmillan, 1964, p. 279

incurred displeasure for such performance appears to be banishment to a comparatively minor post with no loss in salary. Further promotions may come a bit slower, and some minor fringe-benefits such as more pleasing housing accommodation may be temporarily lost, but 'victimisation' in Nigeria even under the deposed politicians did not extend to loss of job and income for senior career professional and administrative civil servants.

Such banishment to less pleasant posts will probably be temporary if the civil servant has been reasonably sound and discreet. Many a minor post has become a major post because a big man filled it. There is room for improvement of performance throughout nearly all of government in Nigeria, and there is useful work to be done in every post. If the sound but banished civil servant continues to perform well in the eyes of his colleagues, and especially if his 'opinions' turn out to be reasonably sound, he may well return to the 'corridors of power' before too many years pass away.

Knowledge is not necessarily power, especially if it is not put to positive and prudent use. However, in the public service, knowledge imposes both responsibility and obligation on the senior civil servant to at least attempt to assist in the exercise of the policy-decision-making power. The Nigerian career civil servant now clearly has this responsibility and obligation to a greater degree than ever before.

12

The responsibilities of the higher civil servant in Nigeria

E. U. Essien-Udom

Hitherto, if one looked up the literature on a number of developing countries (and there are a large number of them in Africa) one would find that a great deal has been said about politics and very little about administration. It is not by accident that a recent book[1] has nothing to say on administrative studies in Africa. So far, we have been attempting to deal with our own problems by applying rules developed elsewhere and in different political cultures and contexts. Thus, if we can start some kind of real dialogue, in the course of time a fund of trust and goodwill can be created between the public servants and the academicians. In turn, this would permit the academician to participate more fruitfully in building up administrative studies in the developing countries. The latter would have access to the necessary documents, which, used discreetly, could throw more light on the problems of administration in societies which are experiencing rapid changes or in 'societies in transition', as others prefer to call the developing countries. These studies would, in turn, be of some value to the administrators and other policy-makers as well. In turn, if the demands of official business would allow, more use could be made of the higher civil servants in providing the various departments of government or political science in our universities with some instruction in such fields as public administration,

[1] *The African World: A Survey of Social Research* (1965), ed. Robert A. Lystad, Frederick A. Praeger, New York

public finance, and diplomacy. I am sure that there are other ways in which academicians and administrators could be of mutual benefit.

I want to suggest that politics is inseparable from administration (of course, we should require a number of case studies to show that this general proposition is correct) and that the distinction between the politician and the higher public servant, as policy-maker and policy-executor respectively, exists more in theory than in practice, especially in the developing countries. The higher public servant ought therefore to be a man of enormous personal integrity—a man of principle—and if he is not a man of great vision, at least he should not be a man without vision.

Of course, there are great diversities among developing countries—diversities in their political systems, ranging from monarchies to liberal democratic states such as India, from quasi-feudal states such as Ethiopia to quasi-socialist states such as Guinea. Most of them have recently emerged from colonial rule; all are economically and technologically backward; all suffer from a shortage of high-level manpower. Nevertheless, all are bent on overcoming their economic backwardness; but most are held back, and for many years will be held back, by archaic traditions which vitally affect not only their economies but also their public administration. Just in passing, one may notice that where the kinship system (or clan organisation) has a great deal to do with the organisation of social life, it can be a source of nepotism and corruption in public life, especially in the recruitment and promotion of men in the public service. Above all, the public service in the developing countries, inherited as it is from the colonial administration, is weighted in favour of habits of doing things peculiar to a different political setting, a different historical situation and a different stage of economic development. It invariably carries over its traditions of the departing colonial overlords, traditions suitable to a government whose primary preoccupation was with the maintenance of law and order rather than the promotion of the material and social welfare of the colonial subjects. The imperial civil servants' traditions, ranging from unresponsiveness and indifference to the demands of the public for efficiency and courtesy right down to the tradition of taking tea at a certain hour in the morning (which in the developing countries can extend to two hours or three hours every day), certainly affect the quality of public administration in a developing society.

Because all developing countries are trying to improve the material conditions of their peoples, the higher public servant should be committed to a developmental ideology, even when this is lacking in the political leadership, as is often the case. He should be infused with such an ideology because, in a very real sense, the higher public servant is a leader of men in his ministry, in his department, or in the public corporation. As a leader, he should be interested more in the achievement of goals than in that status-preservation which is sometimes the preoccupation of higher civil servants, and he should be able to pass on these aims to his subordinates.

Two patterns emerge in the relations between politics and administration in developing countries. First, when the political leadership is committed to a developmental ideology and achievement of goals, the higher civil servants seem to be committed to the *status quo* or to gradual change. This is especially so in countries where the indigenous public service had been relatively long established before the politics of independence set in. I believe that this type of public servant ought to be retired by a political leadership that is bent on development. At least, if he is not retired he should not be placed in a position of undue influence on developmental policies. Such public servants are useless both to politicians and to the public as a whole.

The second pattern is to be found in countries where both the higher civil servants and the politicians emerge about the same time. The politicians are often, on the average, a bit older than the public servants. Hence, a conflict of generations arises. The politician is likely to be committed to narrow interests and gradual change. The public servant, more radical and committed to a developmental ideology, becomes frustrated by the narrow purposes and interests of the politician. But because of his secure income and economic comfort, such a public servant may be gutless, or rather may lack the personal integrity which would inspire him either to provide honest and courageous guidance to politicians or to resign, or even be sacked if the rules of the public service permit it. I am sure the worst that can happen to him is transfer to another ministry. I am advancing the view that it is no excuse to say that the politician has all the power and that therefore, willy-nilly, when the views of the public servant clash strongly with those of the politicians, especially in the case of conflicting visions of society and what is good for society, the civil servant must stay on. What I am trying to suggest is that politics and administration are extremely intimate in developing countries; that the type of civil servant required in these countries must differ considerably from the conception of his role in the classical model. This does not mean that public servants should replace the politicians. It simply means that they must view themselves more as partners in nation-building and development, rather than as boss and servant. With tact, the public servant can do more than carry out senseless policies. He can decisively influence policy-formation. I suggest that he should be prepared quietly to resign, to request transfer from his ministry, or to seek a job outside the government when he seriously believes that his vision and principles are in conflict with those of his partner. If he resigns, he should then be free to explain his views to the public. I do not accept the view, therefore, that public servants are less citizens of a country than the politicians are or that professors are more citizens than are public servants and politicians.

13

Alternative administrative arrangements: the experience of French-speaking West Africa

John A. Ballard

In dealing with the relationship between politics and administration, an observer rapidly becomes aware of the difficulties of trying to make general statements about complex phenomena. It is not easy to define in any adequate fashion the interrelationships of politics and administration in one region of Nigeria, let alone compare the patterns of relationship that exist or existed in the first republic within the various regional and federal governments. Much clearly depended on the competence, character and interests of individual politicians and administrators, particularly during the formative period of rapid constitutional and political change. The same can be said with even more force about French-speaking West Africa, where after 1958 nine states followed their own separate constitutional and political roads, developing systems which differ radically in many respects, though all of them have retained something of their common heritage from French colonial rule.

Given the difficulty of treating all major aspects of politics and administration in these nine states, I have chosen to examine two features in French administration which have been adapted for use by the independent régimes of French-speaking West Africa. The first of these features is the ministerial secretariat, the mixed political and administrative body which has many of the functions of the British permanent secretary in linking together elected politicians and career administrators. The second feature is strongly centralised control over local government. Both of these features offer sharp contrast to British tradition and they may suggest alternatives to present practice in Nigeria.

Ministerial secretariats

France has a long tradition of bureaucratic stability paired with an almost equally long tradition of political instability. As a result the public service in France has a store of prestige and competence which has tended to make it difficult for politicians, unsure of their own political strength, to control effectively the direction and execution of public policy. In addition, within the public service the French have never established a separate administrative class to deal with problems of administrative coordination. Instead, the technical services have developed their own administrative specialists and have guarded jealously their separate identity. As a result, the political minister, confronted with a ministry containing several self-contained departments, has had to create his own instrument for political and administrative coordination. This instrument is known as the ministerial 'cabinet' or secretariat.

The primary job of the ministerial secretariat is precisely that of bridging the gap between politics and administration, serving as the eyes and ears of the minister in both fields. Except in a few major ministries the minister is limited to a secretariat of ten members, selected from the public service or from business, the universities or politics, and chosen for their competence and for the minister's personal confidence in them. Politically, certain members are responsible for the work of a British minister's parliamentary secretary and private secretary, for the minister's relations with his party, his constituents, and interest groups. Administratively, other members do the work of a British permanent secretary, and this is particularly the domain of the Director of Cabinet, whose job is 'to coordinate, to arbitrate and to impose (as far as he can) the minister's point of view on the active administration'. Hence the Director of Cabinet must have the confidence of the higher civil servants in the ministry and is usually chosen from among the senior and widely experienced members of the prestigious corps of financial and legal specialists who are a substitute in certain respects for the British administrative class.

Finally, the ministerial secretariat in both its branches serves as a brains trust at the disposal of the minister. Since the organisation and functions of the secretariat are entirely in the hands of the minister it is a flexible instrument, and several of its members are normally generalists or specialists available for assignment to any tasks which may arise. It is perhaps in this respect that the secretariat is most fruitful and unlike its British counterparts, for it can import new blood into a ministry, both to invent fresh approaches and to impose priorities on the administration, strengthening the influence of the minister both in policy and in routine administrative matters. In fact, because appointments to ministerial secretariats tend to provide broad training and give responsibility to younger administrators or to aspiring young men outside the administration, these appointments attract many good candidates from which a capable minister can mould an excellent team.

The adoption of ministerial cabinet arrangements in French-speaking Africa had, of course, to await the institution of ministerial government in 1957. Directors of cabinet were usually chosen from among the more sympathetic young French administrators, while the political positions within the ministerial cabinets were primarily reserved for party patronage. Since the French failed to provide administrative or technical training until very late, most states were very slow to Africanise their directors of cabinet or, where these posts were Africanised, administrative power remained very firmly in the hands of French department heads. Even today, there is considerable reliance in most states on French technical advisers both attached to ministerial cabinets and backing up African department heads.

Even before independence in 1960, the development of governments under the control of strong presidents or strong parties had given rise to one-party rule in Guinea and Mali, and one-man rule in most other French-speaking West African states. This has had a clear impact on the power and responsibility of both ministers and their secretariats. There has been a general tendency to concentrate decision-making, both political and administrative,

F

in the office of the president, and this office has normally swollen to include an all-powerful director of cabinet advised by several French and African counsellors who provide the president with a super-ministerial cabinet. The prestige and powers of political ministers have shrunk and have been revived only in those states in which young trained African administrators and technicians have been absorbed into the council of ministers. These are men who are able to deal with the administration on its own terms and who have begun to act as permanent secretaries under the president as sole minister, somewhat in the fashion of French ministers of the Fifth Republic under de Gaulle. The tendency within ministerial secretariats themselves has been for each president to look upon it as a legitimate area for placing men of his own choosing, and it is a rare minister who has a free choice in staffing his own secretariat beyond his immediate private secretary.

The experience of the various states is too inconsistent and insufficiently studied to permit further generalisations, but a few of the advantages and disadvantages of the ministerial secretariat should be apparent from this short survey. The obvious advantages lie in the flexibility of the secretariats and their capacity for recruiting talent from all walks of life, providing fresh blood at the top of the administration. The system presupposes, however, a large reservoir of trained men inside and outside government, something which few African states can boast. In addition, whereas in France the ministerial secretariat helps to redress the balance between weak politicians and strongly entrenched administration, in Africa it is the civil service which may need to safeguard its own integrity through the maintenance of a clear boundary between political and administrative posts.

Control of local government

Since the days of Napoleon, and even under earlier royal government in France, there has been a continual bias in favour of administrative centralisation and against the existence of local autonomous authorities. The original justification for this was the necessity to develop royal authority over autonomous provinces and fiefdoms in France, but since the Revolution of 1789 there has been an additional justification in terms of the need to impose equality among all French citizens by providing the same form of impartial government throughout France. Hence France is divided into ninety administrative regions, known as 'departments', each governed by a prefect who serves as the agent of the Ministry of the Interior and of the French government as a whole, by which he is appointed. As sole legal representative of the State in his department, the prefect in principle has administrative authority over all local officials of other ministries. In fact, there have been efforts, frequently successful, on the part of technical ministries to free their agents from administrative control by establishing their own regional groupings of departments, but the traditional bias in favour of a single centralised administrative hierarchy has tended to restore the prefect's position as general administrator with authority over all government affairs in his department.

This centralised hierarchy was easily adapted for use by the colonial administration. In French West Africa a governor-general at Dakar was the supreme political and administrative agent of the State and of the French government, and governors of individual territories, like prefects, had authority over the specialists in education, public works, medicine, agriculture and other fields who served within their domain, though there were frequent disagreements with the general directors of technical services who served directly under the governor-general at Dakar. The same centralised control continued at the regional level within territories, where the *commandant de cercle*—equivalent to the resident in Nigerian colonial administration—served as chief political and administrative officer and coordinator of the activities of various technical services in his region.

The bias against local autonomy of any sort meant in France that although there were elected local government and municipal councils these had in fact very limited powers and served under the tutelage of the prefect. In the French colonies, there was even greater reluctance to allow local institutions to develop, and this meant that there was no encouragement for a system of native administration resembling that of indirect rule. Rather, centralised direct control of all government activities reduced most traditional chiefs to the role of tax collectors and labour-recruiting officers. There was no serious attempt to establish local councils, even on an advisory basis, and after the creation of territorial legislative assemblies in 1946, political activity was focussed at the territorial level and tended to cut off any development of popular local institutions. During the last years of colonial rule, elected municipal councils with their own budgets were established, and there were half-hearted attempts to create elected rural councils and cooperative bodies. But these never really got off the ground, and even the municipal councils were supplanted by agents of the central administration after independence.

The new independent states have taken over the centralised administrative system that they inherited from French colonial rule and have, with relatively minor reforms, kept it intact. Government outside the capital cities rests largely in the hands of prefects, who are chosen both for their administrative ability and for their political loyalty. In states with active political parties, such as Guinea and Mali, there has been some difficulty in separating out the authority of prefects from those regional party officials, but the prefect has tended to gain the upper hand as direct agent of the president and council of ministers, just as the council of ministers has in most cases gradually obtained precedence over the national party executive. In other states this conflict has not arisen and prefects have often become the unquestioned spokesmen of the presidency and government in their regions, combining the functions in Nigeria of provincial commissioners and provincial secretaries but without competition from traditional local government institutions.

The problem of coordinating economic and social development outside the major cities has been complicated by the shortage of technical manpower. In an attempt to decentralise the accumulation of technical expertise in the capitals, some states have experimented with super-regions under super-prefects who have their own staffs of technical officers working at a regional level. These probably resemble in many respects the Area Development Agencies proposed in the February 1966 issue of *Nigerian Opinion* as a means for coordinating regional development administration.

There are obvious advantages for coordinated development through the institution of central government administrative officers in each administrative region, and in attempting to achieve national integration any government is likely to prefer dealing with local problems through its own political and administrative agents. The major disadvantage of centralised control and the absence of autonomous local institutions is their failure to harness local popular energies to the solution of local problems. It may not be impossible to link together prefects of area development authorities with local government councils in a fruitful, cooperative relationship, but as yet there is no state which has succeeded in establishing a stable arrangement of this sort. An additional and related problem in giving wide powers to prefects or their equivalents has been the tendency to recruit these men from a narrow educated élite which has begun to have class interests of its own quite different from those of rural populations. The experience of several French-speaking African states with individual prefects has not been entirely happy, and several have been replaced for exploiting their posts dishonestly.

Conclusion

It is a bold man indeed who will advise that institutions be imported from one political system to another, but the study of foreign institutions does suggest a number of technical problems and possibilities. By observing closely the workings of administrative machinery borrowed from France, in a West African environment and in societies with problems and aspirations similar to those of Nigeria, it may be possible to identify in advance the probable advantages and disadvantages of specific administrative reforms. French-speaking West Africa, with its nine different variations from a basic administrative model, may well prove to be a useful testing-ground for proposed political and administrative structures.

Part VI

Conclusion

14

The future of Nigerian administration

Adebayo Adedeji

During the past fifteen years or so when politicians have become actively involved in the administration of the country, what have been their relations with the civil servants? Are they those of masters and servants? Or have politicians and senior civil servants worked as equal partners? In any country, and particularly in a developing country, the politician and the bureaucrat are of strategic importance. The politician must provide leadership. To do this effectively he must have a vision of change and the gift of making the people see that vision through his own eyes. It is, however, the civil servant who must not only bring the vision down to earth and translate it into practicable policy but also ensure its proper execution once the policy has been accepted. To what extent have civil servants in Nigeria been allowed by the politicians to discharge their functions with a reasonable degree of freedom? In the administrative process, what is the *modus operandi* between the politician and the civil servant?

Very little information has been available about the interaction of politics and administration. The Nigerian civil servants are seen, not heard. Whether or not there have been serious disagreements between them and the politicians over vital issues of state is unknown to the public. The post-Independence events, which culminated on January 15th 1966 in the handing-over of the reins of government to military authorities, turned these questions from academic to topical issues. It was in order that these issues could be discussed frankly and realistically that a programme con-

taining public lectures and symposia was arranged by the Institute of Administration, University of Ife, two weeks after the
January 15th coup. The participation of senior civil servants in
this programme both as speakers and as members of the audience
brought enlightenment and realism to the discussions. The
response of civil servants was tremendous. Not only did they
attend all the sessions in large numbers, they participated fully
in the discussions that followed the lectures and symposia. Five
of the lectures were given by senior civil servants and the speakers
in the symposia were all civil servants.

The texts of these lectures and symposia are contained in the
preceding chapters. Chapters 1 and 2 provide the general background to the discussions which follow. Chapter 1 describes,
quite briefly, the evolution, organisation and structure of the
Nigerian Civil Services. The particular form of hierarchical
structure in these Civil Services and the way they are divided into
classes have given rise to some of the basic problems in the public
service of Nigeria. The one has tended to reduce administration to
a routine process, and the other has brought about incessant and
sometimes acrimonious inter-class struggle.

Politics, administration and the higher civil servant

The characteristics of politics in relation to administration in
Nigeria are analysed in Chapter 2. The intensity of political
activities and the high and rising demand for government services
make the civil services the focus of party political activities.
Although the relations between the ministers and the civil servants,
particularly the higher civil servants, were harmonious up to the
time of Independence, difficulties arose soon afterwards. These
difficulties were most noticeable in the Western region, where as a
result of disunity in the rank and file of the ruling party, the Action
Group, a new political party consisting mainly of the dissident
members of the Action Group, formed an alliance with the
opposition party in 1962. This alliance later became the Nigerian
National Democratic Party (NNDP). This party showed a lack of
sincere commitment to the advancement of the social and economic

well-being of the community. Instead, it pursued a single-minded policy of maintaining power and regarded many higher civil servants with suspicion, if not open antagonism. Its ministers interfered with routine administration and the execution of policy. Just before the coup, these ministers were planning to place the management of the civil service under direct political control. They also exploited the disunity among the rank and file of the civil services and the inter-class struggle between the administrative class and the professional and executive classes to their advantage. And even within the administrative class, the lack of an *esprit de corps* was duly exploited by the politicians.

It is in the light of these circumstances that the outlook of particular groups of civil servants becomes so significant. The case of the professional officers is made most eloquently in Chapters 6 and 7, while that of the administrators is made in Chapters 10 to 12. The rationale behind the setting up of an administrative class in each public service has been that the officers in this class will, by their education and training, have a breadth of vision and knowledge of public affairs and policy which professional officers do not and cannot be expected to possess. The administrative officer will, therefore, relieve his professional colleague of responsibility for policy formulation and general administration. However, the professional officer contends that this has not worked out in practice; that he still has to perform a good many of the functions which the administrative officer is supposed to have taken off his plate. He has also become increasingly impatient of the administrators' unwillingness for change and experimentation; his subservience to rules, regulations and precedents; and his negative approach to problems, particularly issues affecting the professional officer. The professional officer also resents the centralisation of powers in the Treasury or the ministries responsible for finance establishments and personnel matters.

The administrator, of course, thinks that the criticisms made by the professional officers are unjustified. He resents the suggestion that he follows rules and regulations rather blindly, that he is a 'slave' of precedents, that he lacks experience and is nothing more than an amateur. While he agrees that laws are made for men, and not vice versa, he does not think he has any alternative but to apply the rules and regulations as they stand until they are modified or abrogated. He believes that what the professional officer really wants is licentiousness—the freedom to do whatever he likes, when he likes, without regard to General Orders, Public Service Regulations, Financial Instructions and the innumerable Treasury and Establishment Circulars, and the agreed principles on which all these rest.

I may perhaps have exaggerated the standpoints of both the professional officer and the administrator. But the above does not seem an unfair summary of the debates in the preceding chapters and the heated discussions which followed each of the lectures and symposia. One thing which is clear from all these discussions is that the relationships between the two classes need to be re-examined, and that administrators need to become more professional in their field than they have been in the past. The days of the amateur generalist administrator are gone. Administration has become professionalised, and Nigerian administrators must acquire the necessary specialised skills and training if they are ever going to win the respect of their colleagues in the professional classes. We shall say more of this later in this chapter.

With regard to the relations between the politicians and the civil servants, some of the discussions were very critical of the role of the senior civil servants in Nigeria since Independence. Most of the young men and women who took part in the programme had only recently completed college education and had taken up careers in the public services. They were most critical of their older colleagues who they thought had let them and the nation down by being too willing to be the politicians' servants rather than their colleagues. They also lamented the lack of candour and adequate sense of *esprit de corps* in the relations of these senior civil servants with each other.

For a country whose public services are reputed to be among the best in Africa these criticisms may seem unfair. The Nigerian public services have withstood rather gallantly the strains and stresses which the political difficulties of post-Independence years have brought in their train. Nevertheless, there can be no doubt that these public services are far from being perfect and that a number of individual senior civil servants did warrant these strictures. The public was coming to the view, just before the January 1966 coup, that some senior civil servants were just as culpable as the politicians. In fairness to these civil servants, it should be pointed out that, unless politicians were willing to observe the rules of the game, there was very little that civil servants could do other than resign their appointments. Given the limited employment opportunities currently available in the country and the fact that the Federal and Regional Governments are directly and indirectly the major employers of labour, a senior civil servant who dared offend a minister under the first Republic might run the risk of remaining permanently unemployed.

The underlying assumption in all the discussions in the preceding chapters has been that the military régime which came into being on January 16th 1966 will be of relatively short duration. The military governments at both federal and state levels have said, again and again, that the military régime is a corrective one, and that, as soon as the necessary reforms have been made, and as soon as a new constitution agreed upon by the people has been promulgated and the first elections held under such a constitution, they will willingly hand the reins of government back to politicians. Sooner or later, therefore, politicians will be back in the saddle. Unfortunately, the civil war forced on the country by the attempt of Eastern Nigeria to secede from the rest of the country diverted for some time the attention of the military rulers from their main obligation of cleansing the country's public life.

It is most essential for the sake of the country that the military government should not fail as a corrective régime. If it fails, and the soldiers give up the reins of government without correcting some of the past excesses of the politicians, as has happened in some other countries, the politicians would come back unrepentant. And all the lessons of the past fourteen years would have been lost. We shall, therefore, continue to assume that military rule will be a resounding success—a corrective régime that will lay a firm foundation for an honest, responsible, responsive civilian administration in Nigeria.

In the light of the country's experience since 1952, and more particularly since 1960, the *modus vivendi* between the politicians and the civil servants needs to be carefully spelt out. The relationships between politics and administration being so dynamic, it would be extremely difficult to lay down a set of rules which should govern these relationships. Yet, unless such rules exist and are observed, the politicians may soon become arrogant, intolerant of criticism, indolent and corrupt. The senior civil servants, on their part, may be blackmailed into a state of docility, nonchalance and even servility. The old order will have been completely restored!

Most of the rules we have in mind are probably no more than codes of behaviour. They cannot be formalised, nor do they need to be. Nevertheless, there should be a gentleman's agreement to observe them most scrupulously. The few of them that are capable of being codified and written into the country's constitution or laws should be so written.

In Nigeria, as in other developing countries and particularly those in Africa, the major tasks for government are to maintain stability and promote rapid economic and social development. Both of these tasks call for the right type of political leadership—dynamic, dedicated and development-oriented. The development process has to be induced, and the maintenance of political stability and of law and order is primarily a political function. The misfortune of the first Republic was that politicians failed dismally to provide the right type of leadership. Although they paid lip service to economic and social development, they were more interested in pursuing their own selfish ends and in amassing wealth at public expense. It is to be hoped that, in future, politicians will accept their role as the catalytic agents for bringing about political stability and providing the type of leadership which will make the people accept the sacrifices that inevitably have to be made if economic development is to become rapid and self-sustained. The new politicians must be men who are able to see where they are taking the country, who can project their image of the future, and convince the people of the merits of working to achieve this goal.

But it is the administrator who must turn the politicians' vision into practicable policies and execute them. It is therefore essential that the administrators should have the right relations with the politicians, and that both should have a proper consideration for the public. The right relationship between politicians and civil servants can only be one of partnership for the achievement of common goals and not one of subordination. The politician must regard and treat the senior civil servant as his partner, and not as a tool to be blackmailed into performing tasks which are not in the public interest. On the other hand, the administrator must regard the politician as a colleague and must not allow himself to be compromised into a position of subordination. As Sir Stafford Northcote and Sir Charles Trevelyan stated in their now historic report of 1853 on *The Organisation of the Permanent Civil Service*, the administrators must possess 'sufficient independence, character, ability and experience to be able to advise, assist, and, to some extent, influence those who are from time to time set over them'.

It is not the role of the administrator to run counter to the politician over major policy. On major policies, the politicians should have their way even when the administrators are convinced they are wrong. But the politicians, for their part, must allow administrators to have their say. They must learn to appreciate that civil servants very often do know better than either ministers or the electorate and that it is their public duty to bring the test of practicality to politicians' enthusiasm.

If, however, senior civil servants are to have the right relations with politicians they must also have the right relationship with each other. There is no doubt that, by their disunity, rivalry, petty jealousies and personal ambition, the higher civil servants made it possible for unscrupulous politicians to turn them against each other and thus render them impotent. This had devastating effects on morale in the rank and file of the civil service. Among the civil servants, particularly among senior administrators, there is a need to develop an adequate *esprit de corps*.

There is thus an urgent need for a code of conduct to govern the relations between politicians and the administrators on the one hand, and among the higher civil servant administrators on the other. In other words, the administrator must be able to work closely with and loyally for the politician. He must be able to harmonise conflicting views and competing interests. He must be able to advise on, and participate in, the determination of policy, and implement approved policies. He must do all this as the politician's partner, which calls for a high measure of integrity, intelligence, imagination and judgement, and a sense of purpose and direction. On the other hand, the politician must recognise that it is his task to provide leadership, to decide on policies and not to interfere with the execution of policies. He is as much a public servant as the civil servant and must, under no circumstances, attempt to re-establish that master-servant relationship between himself and the senior civil servant which was the bane of the post-Independence era in Nigeria.

Leadership in the public service

If the Nigerian civil services are to meet the challenge of the future adequately, they must be properly led. The need for honest, dedicated, dynamic and courageous leadership in each of the civil services is, therefore, as vital to the well-being of the country as good, honest and dedicated political leadership. The success of any organisation in achieving its objectives depends largely on the calibre of its leadership.

The overall leadership of each civil service falls on the Head of Service. Although this is a title which does not exist in all of the country's public services, there is in each of them a senior administrative officer (usually the Secretary to the Government or the Premier) who performs this role. It is to the head of service, by whatever name he is called, that civil servants look for guidance, direction and protection against the whims and caprices of politicians. It is he who, as the chief adviser to the government, advises the head of government on civil service matters. He administers the service and coordinates the work of permanent secretaries, particularly with regard to policy issues. The promotion of harmonious relations among the various classes and the maintenance of discipline and high staff morale are his primary responsibility.

To succeed in his task, the head of the service needs the

unalloyed loyalty of his colleagues and the unstinted support of the head of his government. Without the cooperation and loyalty of his colleagues, it will be most difficult, if not impossible, for him to maintain the discipline, unity and sense of direction of the service. And unless he enjoys the full confidence and support of the head of his government, he will not be given that degree of independence in the running of the civil service in purely service matters—promotion, posting, discipline, etc.—which is vitally necessary for the development of a sense of unity and purpose among his colleagues. Once he enjoys such confidence and cooperation, he can depend on the head of government to do everything in his power to ensure that his ministers do not interfere in the administration of the service. The high reputation which the Western region civil service enjoyed as the most efficient service in Nigeria, and as one of the most efficient in Africa in the 1950s, was no doubt due to the excellent qualities of Chief Simeon Adebo, its first head. But it was no less due to the unstinted support which he received from the region's head of government, Chief Obafemi Awolowo. There was no doubt that in those years Chief Adebo was in full command of the service. Political interference in purely service matters was negligible.

But the situation had changed dramatically by 1962. Chief Adebo transferred to the federal civil service in the middle of that year, at a time when the Western region was faced with a serious political crisis which had culminated in the suspension of representative government and the declaration of a state of emergency throughout the region. A successor to the post vacated by Chief Adebo was not immediately appointed. Chief I. O. Dina was made to act as head of service for some time, but he was never confirmed in the post and was soon banished to a comparatively minor post. The post of head of service in fact remained vacant from 1963 to 1966. It was resuscitated only after the January 1966 coup. Little wonder then that the Western Nigeria civil service was in complete disarray at the time of the coup. Morale was at a very low ebb. The sense of unity, purpose and direction which had pervaded the civil service in the days of Chief Adebo was found to be lacking. Instead there was a general feeling of insecurity and frustration.

As Dr Murray points out in Chapter 2, the politicians exploited this situation for their own party political ends. Just before the coup they were planning to place the management of the service under direct party political control.

The public service commissions

The role of the Public Service Commission (PSC) is also most crucial. Each civil service in the country has its own PSC which is responsible for appointments, promotions and the disciplinary control of the staff in the service. A PSC is supposed to be a bulwark of strength to civil servants, and their protector from persecution and unfair treatment. The establishment of a PSC for the federal public service is provided by Section 146(1) of the Constitution of the Federation[1] and similarly by the constitutions of the regions. These constitutions also provide that

(1) each PSC shall consist of a chairman and not less than two or more than four members;

(2) members shall be appointed by the head of State (the president of the Republic in the case of the federal civil service and the governor in the case of the regional services) on the advice of the head of government;

(3) a member of the PSC may be removed from office by the head of State on the advice of the head of government; and

(4) members shall be appointed for five years.

The duties of each PSC are spelt out in the constitutional instrument which has created it. They concern appointments, promotions and discipline, though the power of appointment is circumscribed: the power to appoint permanent secretaries, for example, is vested in the head of State, acting in accordance with the advice of the head of government.

[1]The Constitution of the Federation, Act No. 20 of 1963. The Public Service Commissions were first set up under the Nigeria (Constitution) Order-in-Council, 1954, as advisory bodies to the Colonial Governors.

Members of the PSC are expected to be men of independence, integrity and courage. Unless they are, they will not be able to stand up to the pressures to which politicians subject them. And on their ability to discharge their functions with impartiality, independence and integrity depends the efficiency and morale of the Administration. Yet, they are appointed by politicians and hold their offices at their pleasure. It is, therefore, no surprise that members of the public have expressed some doubt about the independence and impartiality of the PSC. Many people hold the view that the Western region PSC failed dismally to stand up to the politicians when the latter began to encroach on the independence and integrity of the civil service between 1963 and 1966. In fact, their scepticism and suspicion seem to have been confirmed by the fact that one of the first acts of the military government in the West was to retire the then chairman of the region's PSC. A further requirement for the future, therefore, is that the Public Service Commissions should be given an authority commensurate with their responsibilities.

The independence of the various Public Service Commissions could be further strengthened by placing their members on the same footing as members of the judiciary or the Director of Audit. In other words, although they could continue to be appointed by the head of State on the advice of the head of government, they could only be removed if a resolution were passed by both Houses of Parliament (in the case of the federal PSC) or by the legislature (in the case of a state PSC) recommending their removal for failure to perform the functions of their office or for misbehaviour. The members should also not be eligible for reappointment on the expiration of their term.

The problems of statutory corporations

There is little that one can add to the analysis by Bayo Kehinde and Z. O. Okunoren in Part IV on the problems facing the administration of public corporations in Nigeria. However, to the three essential conditions which Mr Okunoren suggests in his paper—a competent and knowledgeable board of directors, an effective organisational set-up, and qualified and experienced management personnel—one must add the urgent need to insulate these institutions from party political control. The evidence which has come to light before the various commissions of enquiry[1] which have been set up by the military authorities since January 1966 shows beyond any reasonable doubt (if there was still doubt in any person's mind) that most of these corporations are the bedrock of corruption, graft and nepotism. Instead of giving the country the best of both worlds, statutory corporations have only succeeded in giving it the worst of all possible worlds.

There is also the problem of the proliferation of corporations in all the states of the federation. For example, whereas the West had only one corporation in 1949, the number had increased to five by 1956 and to eight by 1966.[2] And there is considerable overlap in the functions and responsibilities of these corporations. The Marketing Boards which were set up for the sole purpose of purchasing and marketing export produce have become engaged in direct investments in industry and in making loans to private enterprises—the functions of the Development and Finance Corporations. The Finance Corporation in the West has not only concerned itself with the granting of loans for industrial and commercial development, but also owns equity shares in many enterprises and has established its own industrial and commercial enterprises—the supposed preserve of Development Corporations. It is therefore desirable, both from the point of view of administrative

---

[1] The most notable of these are the tribunals of enquiry into the affairs of the Nigeria Airways Corporation, the Nigeria Railway Corporation, the Nigerian Ports Authority and the Lagos Executive Development Board set up by the Federal Military Government; and the tribunals of enquiry into the assets of public officers and other persons set up by the Western and Mid-Western State Governments.

[2] These Corporations are:
Western Nigeria Development Corporations (formerly Western Regional Production Development Board), 1949; Western Nigeria Finance Corporation, 1955; Western Nigeria Marketing Board, 1955; Western Nigeria Housing Corporation, 1956; Western Nigeria Government Broadcasting Corporation, 1959; Western Nigeria Agricultural Credit Corporation, 1964; Western Nigeria Water Resources Corporation, 1966.

efficiency and of operational results, that the overlapping and confusion of functions and responsibilities among statutory corporations should be reduced to a minimum by a rational and clear allocation of such functions and responsibilities.

Fortunately, the military authorities have shown an awareness of, and indeed concern for, the state of affairs in public enterprises. Thus, the Federal Military Government appointed in April 1966 a Working Party on Statutory Corporations and State-owned Companies under the chairmanship of a retired civil servant, Michael O. Ani. The terms of reference included:

(1)   the reorganisation and re-orientation of statutory corporations with a view to increasing their efficient operations;

(2)   the composition and size of boards of these corporations, and the quality and tenure of office of their chairmen and members; and

(3)   the desirability of having an independent Statutory Corporations Service Commission which would be responsible for appointments, promotions and discipline of senior staff of all the corporations.

The Working Party submitted its report[1] later in the year. And most of its main recommendations are not dissimilar from the suggestions contained in Part IV of this volume. The fact of the matter is that the Nigerian governments are really not necessarily short of good and sound advice on the reorganisation and reforms with regard to statutory corporations. What seems to be lacking is the will to implement these recommendations. One fervently hopes that the military régime will have the courage to undertake the essential reforms and thus give the corporations a fresh start. It is in the national interest that they should. Nevertheless there is one further innovation with regard to the public corporations which could be considered. It is to be hoped that to the presently proposed reforms there will be added the innovation of making mandatory the holding of public enquiries on the activities of

[1] *Report of the Working Party on Statutory Corporations and State-owned Companies* (Federal Ministry of Information, Printing Division, Lagos)

statutory corporations every year. Such enquiries would be like congressional hearings in the United States, except that members of the commission of enquiries should be drawn from outside the legislatures and should be men and women of integrity. The purpose of annual public enquiries is to expose the corrupt practices that are so pervasive in these corporations, punish whoever may engage in them before it is too late, and hence deter the reintroduction of a tradition of corruption. To wait until the overthrow of a governing political party by the exercise of emergency or extra-constitutional power before enquiring into its activities while in office, as is now the case, leaves much to be desired.

The future organisation of the civil services

One problem which has not been considered in any detail is the organisation and structure of the Nigerian Civil Services. Chapter 1 describes the structure of the services and their organisation and raises a number of questions, but, with the exception of Dr Ballard's paper which suggests that something might be learnt from the experience of French-speaking West Africa, the issues have not been further discussed. The present structure of the civil services was, as it were, taken for granted by the other contributors. Yet the recent creation of twelve states out of the former four regions and the federal territory of Lagos adds new dimensions to this problem. There is, first, the problem of constructing a satisfactory career-structure in each of the civil services —state and federal. Second, there is the need to review the class structure of the services. And, third, there is the issue of the proliferation of ministries and departments.

The states have smaller physical areas than the former regions. Their resources and functions are also expected to be more limited than those of the regions. The size of their civil services will therefore be necessarily much smaller than those of the former regional services. It will accordingly be very difficult for each state civil service to construct a satisfactory career structure for each of its classes of officers. And without good career prospects the state civil services cannot expect to attract the most able recruits, nor can they expect from civil servants who lack the inducement of promotion a contented and efficient service. One way of solving this problem is to establish an All-Nigeria Administrative Service and an All-Nigeria Executive Service. Of the general service classes described in Chapter 1, the administrative and executive classes are the two most important. Both classes are responsible for formulating and executing public policy. It is most essential that recruits to these two classes should be among the ablest in the country. By converting them to all-Nigeria services, it will be possible to create adequate career prospects for the officers in the two classes. Both classes will accordingly be attractive to high calibre candidates and will be able to retain their able men. The setting up of these two classes on an all-Nigeria basis will also result in substantial economy and greater efficiency and promote national consciousness and unity among the higher civil servants.

The problem of the proliferation of ministries and departments needs to be looked into urgently. A great deal of scarce financial and human resources has been wasted because of the rapid increase in their number. There is also considerable overlap and duplication in their functions.

In fact, what Nigeria needs now is a full-fledged inquiry into its administrative system. The present structure of the civil services was set up in the fifties, and since then a number of important developments have taken place. Among these are the attainment of Independence, the division of the country into twelve states and, perhaps most important of all, the changing concept and character of the civil services. From being primarily concerned with the maintenance of law and order, the country's public services have become increasingly concerned with developmental administration. Yet their organisations and structures have remained unchanged, and now would be an opportune time for the suitability of the established system to be investigated. One of the most important contributions which the military régime could make to the development of Nigeria's public service would be to appoint an Administrative Reforms Commission to undertake a comprehensive enquiry into the administrative system with a view to considering whether the present system of administration is suited to the new objectives to which government is committed, which would enable the public services to meet the challenges. Such a Commission could not only give worthwhile consideration to the experience of other recently independent Commonwealth countries, such as India and Pakistan, but also investigate the lessons to be learnt from the different administrative systems of French-speaking West African Countries, and of countries such as Yugoslavia where a concern with planned economic development has been of greater importance than in countries whose administrative systems have been modelled on those of Britain.

Conclusion

The papers in this book provide an introduction to some of the difficulties which arise for the Administration as a result of operating in a highly charged political climate. The papers do not provide a comprehensive analysis of the impact of politics on administration, but they do serve to bring into the open the difficulties which are considered by those involved to have been of central importance. As the papers indicate, there is a consequential search for ways to avoid a recurrence of past problems. The advent of military rule has provided an opportunity for all to take stock and to question the established order. One opinion, anyway, is that if the old order is not to return, then the established system of administration must be reformed so that it is able both to withstand corrupting influences and to serve as a more effective instrument in achieving the ends of economic and social development. The nature and extent of such changes is a matter for public debate, and to such a debate this book is intended as a contribution.

Bibliography

French Government
F. Ridley and J. Blondel, *Public Administration in France* (Routledge and Kegan Paul, London, 1964)—the best survey.
Brian Champman, *The Prefects and Provincial France* (George Allen and Unwin, London, 1955)—more detailed.
Brian Champman, *British Government Observed: Some European*

Reflections (George Allen and Unwin, London)—a critique of British administration based largely on French experience.

Government in French-Speaking West Africa

David Hapwood, *Africa: From Independence to Tomorrow* (Atheneum Press, New York, 1965)—a critique of administration and development, with chapters on Senegal and Guinea.

M. J. Campbell, 'Local Government Problems in the New States of Africa: the French-Speaking Areas', in *Local Government Throughout the World*, Vol. 5 (March-April 1966)—the best recent survey.

T. G. Brierly, 'The Evolution of Local Administration in French-Speaking West Africa', *Journal of Local Administration Overseas*, Vol. 5, pp. 56-71 (January 1966)—more detailed, but more legalist than practical.

L. Gray Cowan, 'Guinea', in *African One-Party States*, Gwendolen M. Carter (Cornell University Press, Ithaca, 1963).

A. Zolberg, *One-Party Government in the Ivory Coast* (Princeton University Press, Pricenton, 1964).

F. G. Snyder, *One-Party Government in Mali* (Yale University Press, New Haven, 1965).

J. A. Ballard, 'Four Equatorial States', in *National Unity and Regionalism in Eight African States*, Gwendolen M. Carter (Cornell University Press, Ithaca, 1966).

Index

Hanson, A. H., 105
Head of Service, 147; Adebo,
  Chief Simeon, 22, 73, 148;
  Dina, Chief I. O., 148
Hill, Dr Charles, 78

Ibadan, City of, 18; University
  of, 59
Ife, University of, 141
India, 128, 154
Indirect rule, 135
Institute of Administration, 141
  code of conduct of, 42
Integration of Ministries, Report
  on, 7–8, 77, 89
Interest groups, 34–44; as
  channels of communication,
  37; in implementation of
  government policies, 36–7;
  involvement in party politics,
  43; opposition to by civil
  servants, 39; prey of party
  politicians, 40–41;
  as source of information, 36
Interior, Ministry of, 135
Iron and Steel complex, 48

Judicial department, 83

Kenya, 12

Lagos Chamber of Commerce,
  35–6
Lagos City Council, 112
Lagos Executive Development
  Board, tribunal of enquiry,
  151 n.

Lands and Housing, Ministry
  of, 84
Legislative Council, 70
Libya, 113
Limba-speaking people, 12
Little, Arthur D., 106
Local government, French,
  134–7
Local government advisers, 16;
  see also under individual
  administrations
Lugard, Sir Frederick (later
  Lord), 4

MacNamara, Robert, 121
Macpherson, Sir John, 2
Mali, 136; one-party rule in, 133
Manpower budgeting and
  training, 60
Mid-West region, creation of, 5
Milverton, Lord, 4 n.
Military rule, 45, 118–19, 122,
  123–4, 144, 155
Ministerial cabinet, 131–4
Ministries, see under individual
  Ministries

National Council of Nigerian
  Citizens, 18
National Development Plan
  1962–68, 45–65 passim, 73;
  conflict of interests, 47;
  patronage system, 49, 50
National Economic Council,
  48, 52, 56
National Manpower Board, 54, 61
National Planning, Commission,
  61; machinery, 52–3, 61